SHRINES AND HOMES OF SCOTLAND

I   SMAILHOLM TOWER

SHRINES
AND
HOMES
OF
SCOTLAND

BY
SIR JOHN STIRLING MAXWELL
K.T.

With 200 illustrations

W. & R. CHAMBERS, LTD.
6 DEAN STREET, LONDON W. 1; AND
11 THISTLE STREET, EDINBURGH 2.

First published October 1937
Reprinted January 1938
Reprinted July 1957

PRINTED IN GREAT BRITAIN BY
GILMOUR AND DEAN LTD., GLASGOW AND LONDON

TO
A. M. M.

CONTENTS

CONTENTS

ILLUSTRATIONS

The reference figures in the text indicate the numbers of the Plates

ILLUSTRATIONS

x

ILLUSTRATIONS

ILLUSTRATIONS

ILLUSTRATIONS

xiii

ILLUSTRATIONS

xiv

ILLUSTRATIONS

Illustrations were kindly supplied by Robert M. Adam for Plates 1, 6 (lower view), 8, 15, 16, 17, 23, 26, 27, 28 (upper view), 33, 34, 35, 38, 39, 42, 44, 48, 50, 61, 62, 68 (upper view), 73 (upper view), 79, 82, 83, 84, 85, 88, 90, 92, 94, 95 (lower view), 99, 100, 105, and 116 (upper view) ; by Alasdair Alpin MacGregor for Plates 4, 6 (upper view) and 78 ; by H.M. Office of Works for Plate 2 (upper view) ; by Francis Caird Inglis for Plate 40 ; by Messrs. Lorimer and Matthew for Plate 107.   Nearly all the remaining Plates are from photographs made by the Author.

PREFACE

THIS little book had its origin in a coincidence which occurred four years ago. My daughter asked me for a handy book on Scots architecture, a book which did not then exist. A few days later, while I was wondering whether I dared try to fill the gap, a letter arrived from Mr. Alexander MacLehose asking me to undertake this work. His invitation would not have been accepted so gaily had I then realized my own limitations so thoroughly as I do now. Meanwhile three useful books on the same subject have been published. *The History of Scotland in Stone* by Ian C. Hannah, 1934, *The Fortalices and Early Mansions of Southern Scotland* by Nigel G. Tranter, 1934, and *Scottish Church Architecture* by J. S. Coltart, 1936. I recommend all three to my readers. Another book which they will find helpful is W. Mackay Mackenzie's *The Medieval Castle in Scotland* (Methuen) 1927. Those who wish to pursue the subject further could not do better than consult *Details of Scottish Domestic*

Architecture, Edinburgh Architectural Associa-
tion, 1922, and the *National Art Survey of
Scotland* 1921, etc., of which four parts have
been published and a fifth is now in preparation.
Also the *Reports of the Royal Commission on
Ancient Monuments*.

The best books on the subject are still those
of David McGibbon and Thomas Ross, the
Castellated and Domestic Architecture of Scotland,
five volumes, Douglas 1887 to 1892, and the
Ecclesiastical Architecture of Scotland, three volumes, 1896 to 1897. Both, alas, have been out
of print for many years.

The subject of this book does not lend itself to
neat arrangement since nearly all the buildings
discussed belong to more than one period. Nor
must the reader expect an inventory of old Scots
buildings. Only so many are described as are
necessary to illustrate the development in design
which is the theme of the book.

My thanks are due to many owners of old
houses for allowing me to make photographs, to
Mr. Robert M. Adam for many fine views, to
Mr. Alasdair Alpin MacGregor for others, to
Lord Strathmore for a photograph of his historic
Castle and to Sir Herbert Maxwell for permission

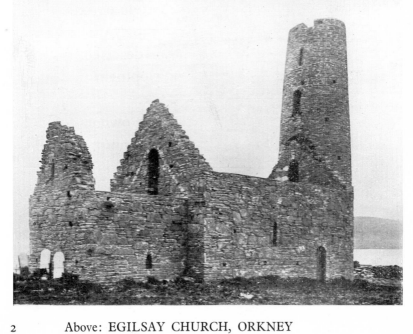

2   Above: EGILSAY CHURCH, ORKNEY
    Below: EARLY CELTIC CARVING AT MEIGLE

3   Above: PROVAND'S LORDSHIP, GLASGOW
        Below: PROVAN HALL, NEAR GLASGOW

to reproduce his charming drawing of Whithorn. The Editor of *Country Life*, Mr. John Matthew and Mr. Caird Inglis have kindly allowed me to have blocks made from the fine illustrations in the Life of Sir Robert Lorimer. I have also to thank His Majesty's Office of Works in Scotland and H.M. Stationery Office for permission to reproduce a plan of Sweetheart Abbey and Mr. J. S. Richardson and Miss M. E. B. Simpson for replies to many enquiries. Not least my thanks are due to Mr. Alexander MacLehose for far more help than any author has a right to expect from his publisher, to Mr. Edward Grant for his friendly assistance in making photographs, and to Miss Ethel Taylor for secretarial work.

The Billings' illustrations are from pen and wash drawings in my possession, which were made for his great book.

J. S. M.

October 1937.

In preparing the second edition I have had valuable assistance from Mr. J. S. Richardson, whose wide knowledge has enabled me to correct a number of errors in the first.

J. S. M.

December 1937.

THE KINGS OF SCOTLAND

Malcolm Canmore - - -	1057–1093
Donald Ban North of Forth -	
Edmund South of Forth -	1093–1097
Edgar - - - - -	1097–1107
Alexander I - - - -	1107–1124
David I - - - - -	1124–1153
Malcolm IV (The Maiden) -	1153–1165
William the Lion - - -	1165–1214
Alexander II - - - -	1214–1249
Alexander III - - -	1249–1286
John Balliol - - - -	1292–1299
Robert the Bruce - - -	1306–1329
David II - - - -	1329–1371
Robert II - - - -	1371–1390
Robert III - - - -	1390–1406
Regent Robert Albany - -	1406–1420
Regent Murdoch Albany - -	1420–1424
James I - - - - -	1424–1437
James II - - - -	1437–1460
James III - - - -	1460–1488
James IV - - - -	1488–1513
James V - - - -	1513–1542
Mary - - - - -	1542–1567
James VI - - - -	1567–1625

CHAPTER I

INTRODUCTORY

The purpose of this book is to provide the reader with a handy account of Scots architecture which it is hoped may increase his interest in the buildings he comes across and help him to determine the period to which they belong. This is easy enough when the building is dated, if not in figures, by initials or coats of arms. It becomes more difficult when it has been altered and still more so when it is in ruins, since the dressed stones, which are often the surest guides to its date are the first to be looted, notably in districts where building stone is scarce. The old builders sometimes brought dressed stones from great distances. Where other guides are lacking the enquirer has to fall back on the plan and general form of the structure. Unless he has some knowledge of the sequence in which these developed he is unable to make use of this evidence. It is a pity that buildings are not signed by their authors like other works of art. Fortunately their purpose is nearly always revealed in their form.

Even so it requires a master mind to classify the buildings of a country when he has to rely mainly on internal evidence. Architectural detail is notoriously difficult to master unless a special study has been made of it. Sir Walter Scott, despite his brilliant historical gifts, tolerated at Abbotsford an ignorant medley of styles which he would have been the first to detect and deride in any other medium. Robert Billings, a trained architect, whose drawings and steel engravings still constitute the most charming record of Scots castles and churches, made the wildest shots at their dates. The truth is that the architecture of a nation not only reflects the broad lines of its history, but also its changing habits and power of satisfying new needs. By these changes it advances and apart from them it cannot be profitably studied. This homely aspect of national life has largely escaped the historian and is actually more fully recorded in buildings than in books.

It was in this spirit that the subject of Scots architecture was attacked by David MacGibbon and Thomas Ross in their monumental work. Their eight stout volumes include descriptions and sketches of nearly every surviving or recorded building erected in Scotland before 1700. They earned our gratitude even more by their intelligent classification of this mass of material. Scots churches fall fairly readily into the recognized categories of architectural style. Not so the castles and domestic buildings, which for many readers have more interest. Here it is not too much to say that these authors found chaos and left order. The present writer is just old enough to remember the delight with which their first two volumes were hailed. This great work has unfortunately been long out of print. Few people have money to buy the rare copies which come into the market or time to study those in public libraries. The present book is an attempt to convey their message to a wider circle. In it their classification is followed and, so far as possible, each of their categories is illustrated by examples.

Among the buildings described by MacGibbon and Ross several had disappeared before their day and were only known to them by sketches and plans. During the forty years which have elapsed since their last volume was published, many more have collapsed or been destroyed. Others, more

3

fortunate, have been strengthened and repaired, some by their owners and many more by the Ancient Monuments Department of H.M. Office of Works, under the Ancient Monuments Acts of 1913 and 1931. The provisions of these Acts are explained in Appendix No. I. It is a typically British piece of legislation, incomplete though cumbrous, but in practice working surprisingly well. It is enough to say here that the administration by the Office of Works of the buildings under its charge has been wholly admirable and that its staff has brought the technique of strengthening and preserving old masonry to the level of a fine art. Such work has been done on a much larger scale in France and other countries, but nowhere so well or with so firm a grasp of the fact that a copy is not the same thing as an authentic document. Besides the privately owned buildings placed in its custody by their owners under the Act, the Department has under its care the buildings which form part of the exiguous inheritance of the Crown of Scotland. For these see Appendix II.

While the Ancient Monuments Act has secured the safety of outstanding buildings, neither the powers nor the funds at the disposal of the Department admit of its extending the same protection to the smaller buildings which are much more numerous and often quite as interesting. The Act is based on the assumption that local authorities will take charge of these and empowers them to do so out of the rates. This provision has in practice been a dead letter. Year by year many interesting buildings are crumbling away. Nearly every year one or two are deliberately demolished to make room for so-called improvements. Our public bodies are terrible vandals. But not always. Some years ago Dundee acquired the curious castle of Claypotts which H.M. Office of Works repaired and keeps in good order for the city. Edinburgh has made Huntly House in the Canongate into a delightful local museum. Jedburgh has preserved the house called Queen Mary's. Aberdeen is considering whether Provost Skene's house can be retained as a feature of the new square facing Marischal College. Alas, such honourable exceptions are rare. Four years ago the town council of Dundee pulled down their old Town House, a renowned work of William Adam which had been the centre of their civic life for nearly two centuries, in order to give more prominence to a singularly ugly new hall. In the course of the same 'improvement' they demolished the Strathmartine Lodging, one of the best examples of a seventeenth-century town mansion surviving in Scotland and the only one of its kind left in Dundee. In any other country these buildings would have been preserved as an integral part of the projected improvement, to which they would have added a distinction now sadly lacking. A few years ago the town council of Stirling replaced by a poor imitation an interesting block of old houses in Broad Street, rejecting a scheme, prepared for them by the Office of Works, which would have preserved the shell of the building and thus kept intact one of the most complete examples of early Scots town planning. A later generation in Stirling has realized that this was a mistake. The present town council has employed an eminent architect to prepare a plan for the improvement of the older streets which will preserve all the ancient houses worth preserving and replace those which are removed by buildings in harmony with local tradition. Glasgow in the nineteenth century allowed its ancient University buildings to be demolished to make room for a railway goods station. The town council more re-

A LINK WITH THE PAST

STEEPLE OF OLD
MERCHANTS' HALL

GLASGOW
STEEPLE OF CATHEDRAL

TOLBOOTH STEEPLE

5

cently sought to remove to a new site the Tolbooth Steeple which for about three hundred years has been the principal feature of the High Street. The pretext was that it had become dangerous. Fortunately this tower had been scheduled under the Act. It has been reconditioned on its old site and, though sadly isolated, is greatly valued as one of the five remaining buildings which remind the visitor that Glasgow is not the mushroom growth which at first sight it appears. The others are the Cathedral, which is happily Crown property, the medieval house called Provand's Lordship, which had the good luck to fall into the hands of a cultivated society, the steeple of the Tron Church and the steeple of the old Merchant's House which is allowed to protrude through the roof of the modern fish market which the Corporation has thought fit to build round it. Even monuments in the depths of the country are not safe. Last year the romantic island castle of Loch Doon was removed to another site to save it from being submerged by a hydro-electric scheme of doubtful utility.

The old buildings are not without friends. There are the antiquarian societies whose transactions are a mine of architectural lore. Quite recently two new movements have come into being—the Association for the Preservation of Rural Scotland, which seeks to maintain the traditional character of the country village, and the National Trust, which has acquired and put in order a number of ancient buildings not sufficiently important to have a claim on the slender purse of the Office of Works. A few public-spirited individuals are quietly engaged in the same work. Thus much is being saved that would otherwise be destroyed, and public opinion is being led in the right direction.

One word of warning. In old buildings it is very difficult to discriminate between good and bad. One's fancy is so much charmed by their antiquity and the adventitious beauty which age confers, that the judgment is crippled. This prejudice is not dissipated but increased by study. Occasionally one comes across men or women sufficiently unsophisticated, discerning and candid to pass an independent judgment on things the antiquarian holds precious. The antiquarian may be hurt by what they say, but if he is wise he will not neglect their verdict. Thus, where all cannot be saved, he will be helped to discard what is doubtful and concentrate on the best.

THE ONLY CURE

The only efficient protection against vandalism disguised as progress is to be found in an enlightened public opinion and such opinion will not come into play till the people of Scotland appreciate the beauty of their old buildings and their historical significance. The present indifference reflects little credit on our very expensive system of education. If this book serves to interest the school teacher and induces him or her in turn to interest the pupil it will realize the author's fondest hope.

CHAPTER II

PRIMITIVE CHURCHES
c. 800–1124

We place ecclesiastical buildings first because they are the earliest of known date. Not only the primitive monastic settlements but most of the great churches are older than any surviving military or domestic buildings, except certain pre-historic dwellings which will be described in a later chapter.

Scotland owed its first known church to St. Ninian, a native of Brittany, who settled among the Galloway Picts at the end of the fourth century. About 397 he built a church known as Candida Casa or the White House, a name still surviving in the place-name Whithorn. If there is any truth in the legend that St. Ninian brought masons from Tours to assist in the erection of this church, it was probably a substantial building and it is a matter of great regret that no part of it survives. It is not even certain whether it stood on the Isle of Whithorn, where the remnants of a later church now stand, or in the town, on the

6   ST. CLEMENT'S CHURCH, ROWDIL, HARRIS
The illustration below shows the MacLeod monument, 1528

7   ST. MARTIN'S CROSS, IONA

site now occupied by the ruins of the Priory. Traces of early Christian occupation are found in the neighbourhood in St. Ninian's cave and on various stones. They take the form of incised crosses of the earliest type with the Greek XR symbol for Christ and inscriptions in Roman lettering. If this cave was actually the retreat of St. Ninian, which there is no reason to doubt, it provides a direct link with him. In these early days Whithorn was an important centre of Christian teaching, but despite the preaching of the men trained there Christianity seems to have taken little root in Scotland in the fifth century.

In Ireland, on the other hand, the faith was already firmly established. In its large and numerous monasteries a wonderful civilization was being developed, destined to produce a wealth of beautiful sculpture both in Ireland and Scotland, as well as exquisite books and metal work, of which some masterpieces are treasured in the national collections. It was from this quarter that the next mission to Scotland came. St. Columba landed with twelve disciples on the coast of Argyll in the year 563 and founded the first Scots monastery on the Isle of Iona. From this centre missionaries were sent out in all directions and numerous churches and monasteries were founded. The ground had been to some extent prepared since for many years Scots from Ireland had been filtering into the highlands and pressing back the Picts. The new missionaries from Iona penetrated still further into Pictish territory, which included all Scotland north of the Forth and Clyde, as well as into the region south of those rivers. Their influence was felt as far north as Orkney, as far east as St. Andrews, as far south as Glasgow and Lindisfarne.

Adamnan records in his life of St. Columba that the first buildings at Iona were constructed of wattles and turf with thatched roofs. They consisted of a church, a cell for the Abbot, huts for the brethren, a refectory and a guest house, all enclosed by a pallisade or by a wall of boulders and turf. This followed the Irish type which was no doubt the model for all the early Christian settlements in Scotland. In Ireland by this time stone had begun to supersede wattle, but the stone huts were of the same beehive shape with rounded corners, built like a drystone dyke and roofed by projecting each course a little beyond the last until the aperture at the top became narrow enough to be bridged by flag stones. In the churches mortar was already in use—the art of preparing lime for this purpose having apparently been introduced into Ireland along with Christianity. The corners of these early churches were made square and the end walls carried up to form gables which admitted of a door at the west end and a window at the east. The same transition from wood and turf to stone took place in Scotland, where the earliest surviving buildings are churches and huts of this type in the western isles. Hermits were a notable feature of the Celtic Church and their cells and oratories are found even in the most inaccessible islands.

The first attempt to embellish these simple structures consisted in the addition of a chancel. In the opening between the chancel and nave are found the earliest examples of a true arch—that is, an arch built with stones radiating from a centre as contrasted with the expedient of overlapping stones described above. Even so these early buildings belong more to the domain of archaeology than to that of architecture. But forces were approaching from another quarter which were to work a complete change and endow Scotland with churches and castles of the first rank.

Thirty-three years after St. Columba landed in

Scotland St. Augustine was despatched from Rome to England. With his mission came Roman building methods, as well as Roman ritual and Roman discipline. As this rival influence spread northwards that of the Columban Church declined and its essentially monastic system was superseded by the Roman system of secular clergy from which are derived our parish priests and ministers. The Culdees or hermit order still lingered on as a separate sect, but before the end of the tenth century the Roman system had been definitely adopted throughout the vast area of the Pictish kingdom.

The long period of 500 years between the coming of these saints and the final adoption of the Roman system under Malcolm Canmore and his English queen seems to be very obscure. From 794 onwards it was disturbed by the Norse invaders. Their buildings were no doubt constructed of wood wherever they could obtain it, as they still are in their own country. The area of natural forest in Scotland was much larger then than it is now. No Norse buildings have, in fact, survived where timber was procurable. A number of their dwellings have quite recently been excavated in Shetland, Orkney and Caithness. To the latter part of this dark period may belong the

ROUND TOWERS of BRECHIN (8), ABERNETHY (9) and
that of EGILSAY (2) in Orkney as well as the earlier
sculptured stones and crosses. These towers
closely resemble the round towers which are so
numerous in Ireland. The Brechin and Abernethy towers are separate from their churches like
the earlier Irish examples, but their fine masonry
and the form of their window openings indicate a
rather late date. The Brechin tower with its doorway of Celtic character seems to have been built
early in the eleventh century after a Danish
invasion. The Abernethy tower has windows of
Norman type and might be a hundred years later.
Each consists of a tapering stone shell with door
well above the ground and ledges to carry
wooden floors. Access to the door and various
stages must have been by ladders. These towers
probably combined the duties of look-out and
strong room. Later they may have been used
as belfries, but the early Celtic bells are all quite
small and evidently intended for the hand. The
Egilsay tower is crudely built, but probably not
very early, since it is joined to the church. It
is of special interest because the old church of
which it formed part was still used for worship in
the nineteenth century, though abandoned some

time before Sir Henry Dryden's visit in 1870, and still remains fairly complete though roofless. It has a nave thirty feet long and fifteen and a half feet wide with mortar-built walls about three feet thick. Over the chancel, which measures fifteen feet by nine and a half feet, there is a room entered by a doorway above the entrance to the chancel and locally known as the 'Grief House'. A similar room or loft is found over the chancel of the beautiful little Norman church of Eastbury in Surrey. It is always difficult to fix the date of these island churches, but from the Norse name of the island (Egilsay—Church Island: Latin *ecclesia* or Gaelic *eaglais*) it may be inferred that there was a church here when the Norsemen occupied the Orkneys in 876. Was it this building? If not— and it seems too elaborate for such an early date —it is unlikely to have been built till after 998 when the Norsemen were converted to Christianity. It was almost certainly built before 1137, when the Cathedral church of St. Magnus at Kirkwall, eleven miles away, was begun in quite a different style. Some churches on early sites were undoubtedly rebuilt later, the Priory Church of ROWDIL (6), Harris, for instance, which cannot be earlier than 1500.

16

BRECHIN
CATHEDRAL
AND
ROUND
TOWER

ABERNETHY, FIFE

MUTHILL, PERTHSHIRE

9 ST. RULE'S, ST. ANDREWS

With these round towers may be grouped five SQUARE TOWERS, all situated in the east of Scotland—St. RULE's (9) at St. Andrews, RESTENNET Priory near Forfar, Markinch in Fife, MUTHILL (9) and DUNBLANE (27) in Perthshire. These are all sites of Culdee settlements and all these towers seem to have been built in the course of the eleventh century. St. Rule's tower has lost its roof, but is otherwise perfect. Those of Dunblane and Markinch differ from the others in having a wheel stair at one corner which does not, however, show from outside. The towers of Restennet and Markinch are crowned by spires of much later date and the Dunblane tower in addition to a spire has had two stories added above the old belfry. The Muthill tower is finished with a gable roof which is probably the original form, though the existing crowsteps may be a reconstruction. The tower of St. Serf's Church at Dunning—also a Culdee site—closely resembles that at Muthill, and though built in the thirteenth century, may be included in this group. It has an elaborate arch leading into the church, of which it always formed part, and a wheel stair which stops half way up. These early towers, with their delicately tapered lines or slightly diminishing stories and their nicely proportioned belfry windows, deserve study from an artistic as well as an archaeological point of view and provide admirable models for the smaller churches of to-day.

The sculptured stones (2, 7) of this period follow much the same lines as those in Ireland, except that in Scotland more of them were designed to stand erect and were, therefore, sculptured on both sides. There is also in Scotland more variety and elegance in the form of the crosses and a more frequent use of figure subjects. The earlier ornamentation consisted mainly of beasts and interlaced ornaments, with symbols which still await explanation. In the later examples foliage plays an important part in the designs. Both types are of great beauty. Modern imitations are numerous and some are very good though many suffer, like most work of our day, from a too mechanical accuracy. It is difficult to believe that the last word has been said in this fine order of design. It was common to the whole Christian world at this early period and from the Greek and Armenian churches found its way into Arabic art. In the Highlands of Scotland it persisted well into the sixteenth century.

CHAPTER III

ROMANESQUE PERIOD—EARLY ABBEYS AND PARISH CHURCHES

c. 1124–1214

We have now reached the period when the great Abbey churches began to be built. Their splendour is evidence of the extraordinary power and wealth of the Church in the Middle Ages and of its intimate connection with the Crown. The close resemblance of these buildings to those of similar or slightly earlier date on the Continent illustrates the Church's universal character which transcended national boundaries to a degree which would be surprising even in these days of rapid transport. The influence of the Church in the Middle Ages will be better understood if it is remembered that quite apart from its spiritual authority it had almost a monopoly of learning and culture, that it owned land on a gigantic scale and was a pioneer in agriculture, at that time the only industry of any importance, and that it made itself responsible, in theory at least, for many functions now performed by Government, such as education and the care of the poor. The monasteries, already very numerous in the twelfth century, provided the machinery by which most of these functions were performed. Their records in Scotland, meagre but frank, are evidence of this. These records deal mainly with questions of discipline and render the delinquents unduly conspicuous, but even a severe critic of the monastic system regards it as 'one of the great formative forces in the social life of the middle ages and at its best the greatest and most beneficent'.*

In Scotland, as elsewhere, the noble simplicity of the original design as conceived by St. Benedict, under which the revenues of the abbey were to be divided equally between the monks, the upkeep of the building and the care of the poor, was soon overgrown by inevitable complications. Despite repeated attempts to revive it whenever new orders branched off from the old, St. Benedict's ideal was never quite recaptured. At the beginning of the thirteenth century there were in Scotland thirty-six Benedictine monasteries of all kinds and thirty-three Augustinian. The

* G. G. Coulton, *Scottish Abbeys and Social Life*, 1933, page 2.

Benedictine group includes the Cluniacs, the Tironesians, the Carthusians, who had only one house in Scotland, at Perth, and the Cistercians or white monks. The Augustinian group embraces the Augustinians or Canons Regular, known as black canons, the Premonstratensians, or white canons, whose special mission was to prisoners, the Trinitarians and the two military orders of Knights Templars and Knights of St. John. The mendicant orders, which comprise the Franciscans or Grey Friars, the Dominicans or Black Friars, and Carmelites or White Friars, did not come into existence till the thirteenth century. Their buildings were less ambitious than those of the other orders. At the close of the fifteenth century there appear to have been no less than one hundred and ten monastic establishments of all kinds, of which eighty were founded before the death of Alexander III in 1286. The nunneries were, as a rule, attached to the various orders. As the monastic houses grew in importance many of the parish churches were made over to them by their founders or their successors, an arrangement which added to the growing prestige of the religious orders but did not always turn out well for the parish or the priest, who had to be content with such share of the endowments as the monks chose to allow them. About half the parish churches seem to have been so appropriated. In 1265 the four Abbeys of Paisley, Kelso, Holyrood and Arbroath had acquired one hundred and twenty-six among them. Kelso alone had twenty-seven. The resulting discontent was among the main causes of the Reformation.

Another was the system of commendations. The weakest spot in the medieval church was its finance, and especially the custom of transferring revenues from one establishment or individual to another, which led to endless abuse. Towards the end of the fifteenth century the pernicious system arose of making over the religious houses to laymen 'in commendam'. The lay commendators appointed by Rome to supersede the abbot or prior were usually powerful nobles who had no interest in the monasteries committed to their charge except to secure as much as possible of the revenue.

It is difficult to estimate the numbers of monks. They certainly varied very much. The numbers given by the Reformers seem to be greatly exaggerated. At Melrose the number of monks in

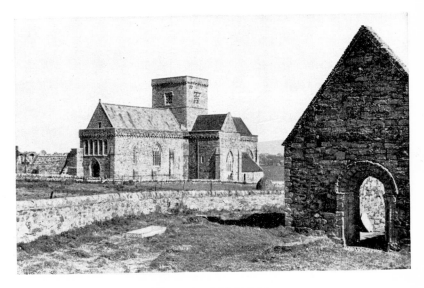

IONA CATHEDRAL

Above: From the hill

Below: From St. Oran's Chapel

FIFTEENTH CENTURY DOOR,
PLUSCARDEN PRIORY

II   THIRTEENTH CENTURY DOOR,
AUCHINDOIR CHURCH

the fifteenth century seems to have varied between twenty and thirty. It had in the earlier centuries been much greater. For a small house thirteen, corresponding to Christ and his apostles, was the usual number. Under the 'commendam' system the numbers were naturally very much reduced. After the Reformation grants were given in perpetuity and the houses thus conveyed became to all intents and purposes the private property of the hereditary commendators, in many of whose families they still remain.

Before the abbeys are described, let us glance at the plan which the buildings usually followed in Scotland, whatever the order. The church was the outstanding feature. The cloister garth round which the other buildings were grouped lay to the south of the nave. It was only placed on the north side when water was not available on the south. It was surrounded by covered walks, one of which was attached to the south wall of the church. At each end of this walk there were doorways into the church but the Cistercians had only the eastern one. The eastern range of buildings abutted against the transept, the various rooms entering from the cloister. Beginning from the transept, the first room was often the

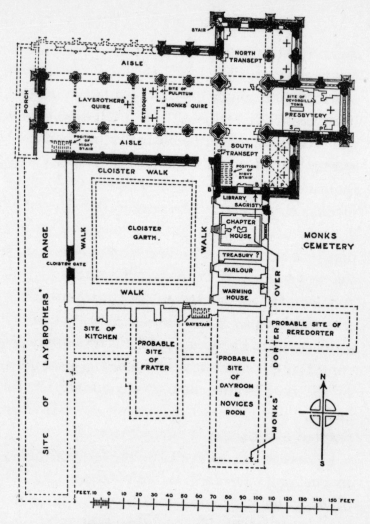

THE ABBEY OF SWEETHEART

A. WALL AUMBRY.
B. BOOK PRESS.
P. PISCINA.

S. SEDILIA.
+ ALTAR SITE.

Dotted lines indicate foundations which have not been exposed.

sacristy, with a door opening from the church. Next came a passage called the slype forming an exit from the cloister towards the east. Beyond it came the chapter house with a handsome door and a window on either side. Next came the warming room, often, but not always, the only room with a fire, except the kitchen. Then the monks' day room. Last came the lavatories if water could conveniently be supplied at this point. The monks' dormitory or dorter occupied the upper story of this range. It usually had direct access to the transept of the church by a stair. The refectory or frater and kitchen were in the south range. The west range was sometimes occupied by the abbot or prior's lodging, sometimes by the novices' quarters or accommodation for guests. The lower story of this range was often devoted to cellars and storerooms.

DUNFERMLINE ABBEY (13–15), the first abbey in Scotland, was founded by Margaret, Queen of Malcolm Canmore, probably soon after her marriage in 1070. This pious lady seems to have made a determined effort to bring the Culdees into the Roman Church. It failed because they were unwilling to adopt the rule of celibacy for their clergy. Of her buildings nothing remains here, but the foundations of a small church below the floor of the existing nave and in EDINBURGH CASTLE (12), in the little chapel still called by her name, the lower courses and possibly the south-west window. The chapel, judging by the chancel arch, must have been rebuilt at least a century after the Queen's death. She died in the Castle in 1093 a few days after King Malcolm fell at Alnwick. The Abbey of Dunfermline as established by Queen Margaret had only the standard thirteen monks, but it grew rapidly in importance. By the end of the fifteenth century the number of monks had increased to thirty-eight and in the intervening period may have been even larger at times. This abbey was reputed to be the richest in Scotland and the palace attached to it was a favourite residence of the Scots kings from Malcolm Canmore to James VI. Elizabeth, Queen of Bohemia, was born here in 1596 and her brother, Charles I, in 1600.

The nave of the church is the earliest of the surviving buildings and the only one which belongs to the period we are now considering. It is a superb example of the Norman style which would do credit even to its home in France, and is, happily, almost intact. It closely resembles

EDINBURGH CASTLE

Above: St. Margaret's Chapel

Below: Half-Moon Battery

North Aisle

West Door

DUNFERMLINE ABBEY

13

the nave of Durham Cathedral, at the founding of which King Malcolm was present and, though not built till after his death, may owe its existence to his conception. It was begun soon after the accession of David I in 1124 and is the earliest of his many churches.

The nave is entered by a fine west door (13) between two towers much altered but probably part of the original composition. That on the left or north side was rebuilt at the end of the sixteenth century. It was designed by William Schaw, master of works to the abbey, and may be regarded as a purely local production typical of its date in Scotland. The other was destroyed by lightning in 1887 and patched up three years later in its present rather bald form. The doorway is a good example of twelfth-century work in Scotland. In England it would indicate a date some fifty years earlier. It has five orders, orders in this sense being the stages by which a doorway or window is recessed into the wall. There is a good Norman door on the north side of the nave partly concealed by a sixteenth-century porch and another of exceptional beauty on the south side.

The interior (15) has the three stories usually

found in large churches. The lower consists of the arcade separating the nave from the aisles. Its arches rest on massive circular pillars, some of which are decorated, like those at Durham, with bold chevron mouldings and spirals. The shallow bases on which they stand and the simple so-called cushioned capitals are typical of their period, as are the mouldings of the arches they support. Above this arcade is the triforium or passage under the aisle roof with an opening into the nave above each of the main arches. Over this again is the clerestory, so called because it rises above the aisle roof and admits of windows. The windows are large single lights with semi-circular heads.

The alterations near the western door reflect trouble occasioned by the flanking towers. The construction of the medieval builders was by no means always sound. When the great western front of Peterborough Cathedral had to be underpinned a few years ago it proved to be devoid of proper foundations. When Paisley Abbey was restored, great cost was incurred in making good the foundations of the pillars which carry the central tower. One of the Dunfermline piers has been rebuilt in a form which suggests work of the fifteenth century, being designed as a group of small shafts in place of one massive pillar. The arches next the door have been blocked with masonry to assist in supporting the towers.

The nave is roofed with wood like Durham Cathedral and most large Norman churches. The aisles (13), which have a narrower span, are vaulted with stone and ribbed, which means that the vaulting is composed of ribs which carry the stone filling inserted between them. On one side these ribs spring from the great pillars of the nave, on the other from responds or pilasters attached to the outside wall. These responds consist of three shafts grouped together, and below the windows the wall is decorated with graceful arcading. All these features are of the best, and deserve careful study.

This building has been described in detail because so few Scotsmen seem to know it. They think of Dunfermline, if they think of it at all, as an industrial town with an historic past which has completely vanished. Many who know the churches of Normandy quite well are unaware that here and at Kirkwall, Jedburgh, and Kelso the Norman style can be studied almost as well as in France.

No visitor should leave the abbey church without glancing at the buttresses (14) added in the sixteenth century to support the thrust of the aisle vaults. The Normans depended on the thickness of their walls to absorb this stress. Their shallow buttresses, probably a survival of the Roman pilaster, are intended more for ornament than for any practical purpose. These sixteenth-century buttresses are quite different. They supply resistance at the critical spot. But what you are asked to note now is their form, which is peculiarly Scottish. A buttress to be effective must project far out from the wall at the base, but as it ascends the projection may be diminished. In England and on the Continent this reduction is usually effected by a few bold steps at long intervals. In Scotland the same result is achieved by numerous shallow steps placed close together.

The choir of Queen Margaret, to which this new nave was no doubt originally attached, was replaced in the thirteenth century by a larger choir with transepts and a central tower. At the eastern extremity a lady chapel—a chapel dedicated to the Blessed Virgin—was built to contain the tomb of Queen Margaret, who was canonized in 1249. The choir with all its splendour was ruined at the Reformation and has since been replaced by a large modern church, to the east of which the foundation of the lady chapel can still be seen, with the remains of the tomb.

At the risk of some loss of chronological order let us examine for a moment the buildings attached to the church, which are typical of those of other abbeys in Scotland. At the close of the thirteenth century they were described by Matthew of Westminster as fit to house three kings with their retainers. The Abbey was burnt by Edward I in 1303 and again by Richard II in 1385, so these buildings had a short life. Only the under building now remains. The monks' quarters were rebuilt after the second fire more or less on the old foundations but no doubt with increased magnificence. The Abbey suffered severely in the Reformation, as we have seen, and what was left fell into neglect and was no doubt used as a quarry. The remnants are extremely imposing. They consist of two walls of the monks' refectory, with its under buildings, two chambers in the adjoining Pend Tower, so called from the arched passage below it through which the road passes, and on the other side of the road, the king's kitchen and behind it again the Royal Palace. These buildings were probably begun soon after the fire of 1385 but they are mainly of the fifteenth century. They are perched on the side of a steep ravine. The site necessitated much under building—always a telling feature in architectural composition—and the result is truly magnificent. The rooms themselves must have been very fine. The monks' refectory or dining hall was over a hundred feet long by thirty broad with a timber roof carried on pilasters which divided it into seven bays. In the eastermost bay is the pulpit from which one of the brethren read aloud during meals. This noble hall was lit by tall windows at the side and at the west end by a larger window filled with fifteenth-century tracery of a type known as Kentish, probably the result of a Canterbury connection. This window may be an afterthought as the Pend Tower, which adjoins it, undoubtedly is, as well as the passage leading to it, which is inserted between the hall buttresses and forms such a picturesque feature of the exterior. A dining room of these proportions for thirty-eight monks may seem excessive, but it must be remembered that the monastery sheltered a number of novices.

14   DUNFERMLINE ABBEY, NAVE AND TOWERS

15   DUNFERMLINE ABBEY, THE NAVE

Guests, to judge from the accommodation provided in other abbeys, must also have been numerous. Among the guests were no doubt the vicars of the numerous parish churches belonging to the Abbey and the missions arriving from time to time from Rome or from English and continental houses.

The vault of the monastic kitchen, later known as the king's kitchen, was supported by pillars and it was on the same generous scale as the refectory. Below it is a room with pillars and vaulting of older type which may have escaped the fires of the fourteenth century. Behind the kitchen are the remains of the palace, formerly the guest-house. This building was probably in the form of a quadrangle. The only side which remains contains the hall and a large room probably used as a drawing room. The hall is about one hundred feet long and the other about fifty. Both have large mullioned windows of later date overlooking the ravine. The under building on which the palace stood was probably the work of Robert the Bruce.

The Abbey occupies a splendid site. The church stands on the hill top. The monastic buildings sit in its shelter to the south at a slightly lower level; the palace still lower and more to the west. The whole pile when it was complete at the beginning of the sixteenth century, supported by massive under building and crowned by the three towers of the abbey church, must have been superb.

Kelso and Jedburgh are two other important Norman churches. The ABBEY OF KELSO (16) was founded in 1128 about the same time as David I began building the nave of Dunfermline. The monks had been brought to Selkirk fifteen years earlier by David I while still Earl of Huntingdon. They were moved to Kelso to be under the shadow of the royal castle of Roxburgh—a famous stronghold of which scarcely any trace now remains. In its new home this abbey became one of the richest in Scotland and for over two hundred years claimed precedence over all others. It suffered very severely in the War of Independence and even more so in the sixteenth century. Its ruin was completed by the mob at the Reformation. In 1559 the Crown took possession of it and it was finally conferred on Ker of Cessford, to whose representative, the Duke of Roxburgh, it still belongs.

We shall not describe these Norman churches

KELSO ABBEY

16

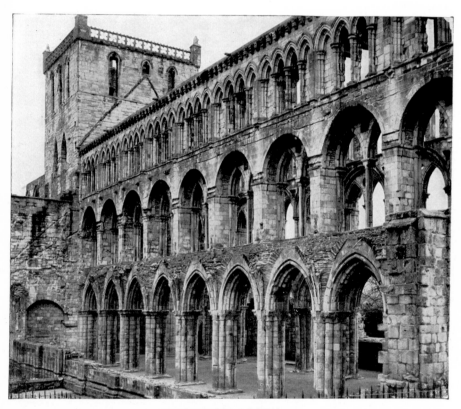

17   JEDBURGH ABBEY

in detail as there is scarcely anything distinctively Scots in their architecture. But the plan at Kelso is too unusual to be passed without comment. In church construction the bay is the recognized unit, a bay in this sense, denoting a unit of the longitudinal design repeated as many times as may be necessary to give a building the desired length. If a church were cut right across from the ridge to the foundation through each pair of the main pillars, each slice would represent a separate bay. At Kelso the choir and main transepts have been destroyed as well as most of the nave. Only the west end of the building remains. It consists of western transepts, each of one bay, with a tower over the crossing beyond which the nave extends one bay westward. This cruciform arrangement of single bays of equal height with a still loftier vault above the crossing is unusual and very striking. When the building was complete the height as compared with the floor space must have been overwhelming and greatly enhanced by the fact that the triforium and clerestory are both treated as continuous arcades. The tower at Kelso is a good example of the transition from Norman to first pointed. The four great piers which carry it—its legs, if we may borrow the word from an eighteenth-century report on Westminster Abbey*—are pure Norman, but the arches they carry are pointed. The transition was more than a change from the round to the pointed arch, as will be seen by comparing the front of the north transept with what remains of the west front. The first is composed of five stories piled one above the other. In the design of the second there is a distinct attempt to treat the front as a single composition with a tall arcade and windows above the great west door crowned by a large circular window in the gable.

JEDBURGH ABBEY (17) is another of David's foundations. It began as a priory in 1110 but was raised to the dignity of an abbey in 1147. Here we find an unusually long nave and relatively short choir. In style it is distinctly later. The circular columns which at Kelso appear rather short and stumpy are here carried up right through the triforium story, which thus assumes almost the appearance of a balcony. The main arches of the nave are pointed, as well as two of those which carry the central tower. The clerestory shows two beautiful types of first pointed design and is perhaps the most satisfactory part

* *Wren Society*, vol. xi, page 10.

of the building. The church was terribly damaged by English invasions from the time of Edward I onwards. Of the choir and presbytery —a prolongation of the choir eastwards without aisles—very little is left and the great legs of the tower have been much altered but their original form has been revealed in recent repairs. This building is in the custody of the Office of Works and has recently been put in excellent order.

The next in date of the great churches is the CATHEDRAL OF ST. MAGNUS at KIRKWALL (18). This is really a Norwegian church, having been built during the Norse occupation. It was begun in 1137, some twelve years after Dunfermline.

Its origin is interesting. At the beginning of the twelfth century the government of Orkney was shared between two cousins, Haakon and Magnus. In 1115 Magnus was killed by Haakon, who seized his portion. Soon after his death Magnus was canonized. His nephew, Ronald, claimed his uncle's portion and vowed that he would build a 'stone minster' in his uncle's honour if he succeeded in making his claim good. He did succeed and this church is the fulfilment of his vow. It is said to have been designed by Ronald's father, Kol.

It is surprising to find so magnificent a building in such an outlandish place and to find it so full of French Norman influence and so rich in lovely detail. Kol must have known Normandy well or brought able assistance thence. The church as first designed was wholly Norman in style. It was fully equipped with nave, aisles, transepts and choir. But this did not satisfy the next generation. The outside buttresses were strengthened and new supports contrived in the triforium to carry the weight of a vaulted roof, a comparatively easy task as the span of the nave is only seventeen feet. At the same time the choir was lengthened and heightened. The result is a church of the first order rendered all the more impressive by the fact that it is the only large building in a bare and treeless country. The interior is equally striking. No one who has seen it ever forgets the first impression made by the length and height of its narrow vista.

The building is Crown property and has lately been restored through a noble bequest of the late Sheriff Thoms. It still has four of its old bells, three of which were the gift of Bishop Robert Maxwell, a member of the writer's family, who held the see in the sixteenth century.

18   KIRKWALL CATHEDRAL

DUNDRENNAN ABBEY

Above: Chapter House

Below: Transepts

This church was served by secular clergy and therefore has no cloister or buildings attached to it. The clergy who conducted its services must have lived in buildings in the chanonry, as we shall presently see was the case in Glasgow.

DUNDRENNAN ABBEY (19) is yet another of David's monasteries. It stands about half a mile from the sea on the coast of the Stewartry in a little valley which is still as secluded though not so remote from the world as it was in 1142 when the second mission of Cistercian monks summoned to Scotland from Rievaulx in Yorkshire took possession of this attractive site. Building began here at least thirty years later than at Kelso or Jedburgh. By this time the transition from Norman to first pointed was almost complete. Some of the windows still have round tops, but this form persisted in Scotland long after it had disappeared south of the Tweed, having evidently a special attraction for Scots builders. We shall see later that it continued to be used even in the sixteenth and seventeenth centuries with little deviation from the original type. This abbey was not destroyed in the wars. The parish worshipped in part of the church till 1742. It was then abandoned and the buildings on which so

39

much care and skill had been lavished became a quarry. Enough is left of the church to show that it was designed with that combination of boldness and delicacy which is the outstanding merit of its period. The cloister lies to the south of the church. It is sadly ruined but the entrance to the chapter house which, as usual, opened from its eastern walk, has luckily escaped. This building seems to be rather later than the church. It shows all the refinement of the pointed style at its best. On its pillars appears the filet, a flat member superimposed on the curved surface of the mouldings and shafts which serves no purpose except that of enhancing the richness of the mouldings by the addition of delicate lines of light and shadow. These thirteenth-century architects did not achieve their effects by chance. Another elaboration characteristic of the period is seen in the cusping of the central doorway on which the remains of lovely carvings of foliage may still be traced.

In this delightful retreat, as guest of Edward Maxwell, the last abbot, Mary Queen of Scots found a brief refuge after the Battle of Langside. Here she spent her last night in Scotland and embarked for England from the little harbour at the mouth of the Abbey Burn. The building is Crown property and well cared for. Its interest for visitors is much enhanced by an excellent guide book which explains the use of the various buildings.

At COLDINGHAM PRIORY (20, 21) the north and east walls of the choir are incorporated in a modern church. This priory, founded in the seventh century by the daughter of one of the Northumbrian kings, was reconstituted by Edgar, son of Malcolm Canmore, in 1098 and assigned by him to the Benedictines of Durham. It remained in their possession till 1509, when it was transferred to the Abbey of Dunfermline. At the Reformation it passed into the hands of the forebears of the Earl of Home, to whom it still belongs. The choir is a notable example of the earliest phase of pointed work. The design was bold and retained much of the Romanesque character, combining this with carved ornament of great delicacy. This is a building which repays careful study. Externally the walls are divided horizontally by flat buttresses into narrow bays and vertically by a string course into two stories. In each bay the upper story is filled by a large pointed window, while the lower contains two

round arches of a blind arcade. At the corners
are square turrets, one of which contains a wheel
stair. The whole is set on a deeply projected
plinth with bold mouldings which give the building a fine air of strength. Evidence of the care
with which the design has been made is found in
the broken line of the string course which is
lowered where it crosses the buttresses and
turrets to improve the proportion of the stories
which would otherwise have appeared too nearly
equal in height. Inside the lower story is occupied by a continuous blind arcade of pointed
arches. The upper story has an open arcade
between which and the windows there is a narrow
gangway. The arches opposite the windows are
much taller than the others. The change of
height is skilfully managed and the result is lively
and pleasing, especially on the side walls where
the taller arches are separated by two of the lower.
The string course on which the arcade rests is
almost level with the string course outside, where
it is lowered on the buttresses. The object in
both cases was probably to divide the stories in
the proportion known as the Golden Cut, which
is approximately five to eight. This proportion
has found favour with the artists of all ages and

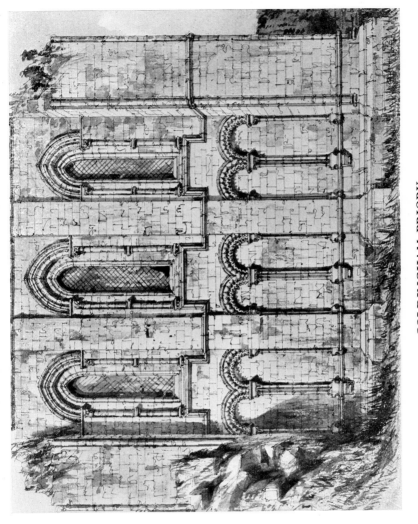

COLDINGHAM PRIORY

21   COLDINGHAM PRIORY

all countries and seems to have some inherent
satisfaction for the human eye. Where it is used
the lesser part bears to the larger the same proportion as the larger to the whole, which may be
roughly expressed in figures as $5 + 8 = 13$. The
relation of the two arcades to each other in the
interior of this church deserves notice for another
reason. On the east wall the central arch of the
lower arcade is immediately below the central
window. This the designer considered sufficient
concession to the demands of symmetry. For the
rest of its course the lower arcade goes its own
way without any relation to the openings above.
This imparts to the design, as the builder no
doubt intended, a vigorous freedom which
would have been killed by more symmetrical
spacing.

DRYBURGH ABBEY (23) is known to British
readers as the burial place of Sir Walter Scott.
No resting place could be more appropriate for
the man, or more beautiful, than this grey ruin
standing among big trees beside the Tweed and
compassed by one of its finest bends. This abbey
belongs to a rather later date than those we have
been considering. It was founded in 1150, three
years before the death of David I by Hugh de

Morville, Constable of Scotland, for White Friars of the Premonstratensian Order. The few remaining arches of the church are pointed and of great beauty. They are surmounted by a low triforium with circular openings. The west door appears to be of much later date, a good example of the persistence of Romanesque design in Scotland.

The monastic buildings belong to the earlier date. They are as usual attached to the south side of the church and surround a cloister garth at a level slightly below that of the church. The eastern range is the best preserved. First comes the sacristy entered from the transept, next a passage called the inner parlour, then the chapter house—measuring forty-eight feet by twenty-three feet—entered from the cloister by a fine doorway flanked by two windows which have no grooves for glass. This noble room, in addition to the subdued light received from the cloister, was lit by five windows at the other end. The gable was here projected to admit of windows facing north and south as well as three facing east, so as to catch all the morning sun. Beyond the chapter house is a room fifty feet long, which was the monks' warming house. It is well planned with three good windows in the east wall and a fireplace opposite. The original doors, one leading into the cloister and the other into an outer court, were both kept well away from the fireplace. A stair in the wall entered from the cloister leads to the dormitory which extends over all the rooms described. The eastern front of this range of buildings is well preserved and is a fine example of its period, devoid of ornament and frankly expressing its purpose, but admirable in the dignity and balance of its design, its fine masonry and telling mouldings.

Before we leave this period let us glance at two of the smaller churches, which still serve the parishes of Dalmeny, near Edinburgh, and Leuchars in Fife. Little or nothing is known about their history but their style indicates the middle of the twelfth century as their probable date. They show the Romanesque style in an advanced stage but without any sign of the transition to Gothic. DALMENY CHURCH (22) is the more complete. It consists of a nave without aisles or vaulting, a small square-vaulted chancel and beyond it a semi-circular apse also vaulted. The arches leading from nave to chancel and from chancel to apse are elaborately carved and their relative size is nicely calculated to enhance the perspective as seen from the west. The south doorway is also a notable composition. The carvings above it are not only interesting in themselves, but arranged by a master hand to meet the constructional demand no less than the aesthetic. Above this door is an arcade of interlaced arches which indicates a late period of Norman work. The masonry, composed of neatly dressed stones, so short as to be almost square, is typical of Norman work in Scotland, as in England and France. The windows—except the centre window of the apse which has been enlarged at a later period—rest on a carved string-course and are admirable both in form and decoration. The whole building, indeed, is a model of consistent design and ornament perfectly applied. A tower seems always to have been contemplated at the west end and one has recently been added.

LEUCHARS CHURCH (22) is more elaborate, but not so complete. Only the square chancel and apse are left. Both are decorated on the outside with two stories of arcading. The lean-to roof of the apse was replaced in the seventeenth or early eighteenth century by an octagonal belfry, graceful in itself, but to be regretted, since it sits

LEUCHARS KIRK

DALMENY KIRK

22

DRYBURGH ABBEY

awkwardly on the older walls and necessitated the insertion of a supporting arch inside the apse.

There were many other parish churches of this date. Remains of them are found at Edrom and Chirnside in Berwickshire, at Cruggleton in Wigtownshire, at Monymusk in Aberdeenshire, at Birnie in Morayshire, and at Duddingston in Midlothian. Others of rather later date are at Uphall and Kirkliston in West Lothian, at Tynningham and Gullane in East Lothian, at Rutherglen and Lamington in Lanarkshire, at St. Blane's in Bute and elsewhere.

CHAPTER IV

FIRST POINTED PERIOD—
THE CATHEDRALS
c. 1214-1285

We have now reached the time when the finest churches of France and England were built. The First Pointed style, sometimes called by the misleading name of Early English, which produced the earlier of these masterpieces, extended roughly from 1150 to 1250. In Scotland, as we have seen, the transition from the round arch to the pointed took place much later and was never complete. Here the First Pointed period coincided with the prosperous reigns of the second and third Alexanders when seventy-two years of brisk trade and unbroken peace made building on a large scale possible. To this period, 1214-1286, most of the Scots cathedral churches belong.

The Celtic churches had their bishops, but under the Roman order the office became of much greater importance when the whole Christian world was divided territorially into sees. Every see had a bishop responsible to the Pope and was divided into parishes in each of which was posted a secular (*i.e.* non monastic) priest responsible to the bishop. The cathedral town was the seat of the bishop and the church derived its name from his cathedra or throne. Its services were conducted by a provost, or dean, and chapter whose establishment, attached to the church, closely resembled that of the abbeys.

When David I became king the parish churches were already numerous, but there were only three recognized episcopal sees in Scotland : St. Andrews, which dated from 950 and later became an Archbishopric, and Moray and Dunkeld, both recently created. In the course of his reign the sees of Glasgow, Aberdeen, Dunblane, Brechin, Ross and Caithness were formed. The cathedral of Ross was at Fort Rose, that of Caithness at Dornoch. Several of these sees had a shadowy earlier existence. That of Glasgow claimed to go back to St. Mungo. Those of Dunkeld and Dunblane had formed part of the old Culdee diocese of Abernethy. The see of Argyll and Lismore was separated from Dunkeld in 1200, but more than three centuries elapsed before the abbey church of Iona became the seat of its bishop in

1507. The see of Galloway had its cathedral at Whithorn. There was a bishopric here in the eighth century, but it was absorbed later by the see of York. It was probably reconstituted in the twelfth century when the priory church became a notable place of pilgrimage. The comparatively modern see of Edinburgh for which the choir of St. Giles's Church did duty as cathedral had a brief but stormy existence. It was established in 1633 as part of Laud's reform, was in abeyance from 1637 to 1661 and finally abolished in 1688.

The bishops were called by the names of their cathedral towns, except those of Ross, Caithness, Moray, Galloway and Argyll, who have always used territorial titles.

We need not discuss here the reasons for the change from the round arch to the pointed. They are discussed in Appendix III. Suffice it to say that the change arose out of the problem of the groined roof which was the outstanding achievement of French gothic. The French builders of the thirteenth and fourteenth centuries pressed the principle of the groined vault to its utmost limit. In their churches the vault is raised to such a height, its weight and thrust are so boldly carried across the aisles by flying buttresses, the

24   ST. ANDREWS CATHEDRAL FROM WEST DOOR

GLASGOW CATHEDRAL

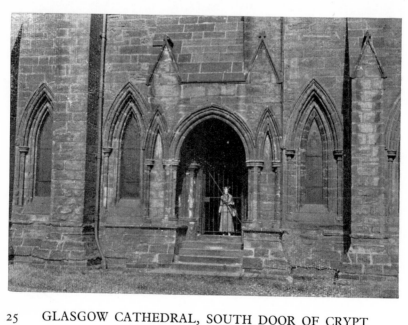

25   GLASGOW CATHEDRAL, SOUTH DOOR OF CRYPT

walls so completely replaced by windows, that, whether seen from within or without, it seems scarcely credible that these airy structures built of comparatively small stones should remain standing. At their best these French churches have a psychological effect which no other type of building has yet achieved. Association no doubt plays its part as it always does in architecture. The fierce Christianity of the Middle Ages is built into the stones and glows in the wonderful glass. But the direct appeal, the appeal of the structure itself, also reaches those to whom Christianity means nothing. To enter the Cathedral of Chartres or Bourges is to leave the outer world completely behind. 'The height, the space, the gloom, the glory'—to quote words which Tennyson used of a less worthy building—overawe the mind and at the same time refresh the eye. The silence broken by rich echoes charms the ear. The multiplicity of parts all bent on one harmonious purpose delights the intelligence. There is nothing in Scotland, or for that matter in England, quite so overwhelming, nor quite so carefully thought out. In the churches of the Ile de France—the district round Paris—every detail of the design expresses its functional purpose. But the limit of safety was more than once over-stepped. The choir of Beauvais, the tallest of all, collapsed before it was finished. Additional supports had to be supplied when it was rebuilt. Where is the line to be drawn between splendour and ostentation? In English work of this period, the function of each part is suggested but not insisted on. The result, if less grandiose, is more restful.

In style the Scots churches followed fairly closely the English models, though smaller in scale and some fifty years later in date. They lack the soaring vaults and wealth of sculptured figures which are found at Westminster and Wells. The transepts are frequently absent or short, with aisles only on the east side. Ribbed vaulting is rare, except in the aisles and over the crossing. On the other hand the Scots churches have certain fine features of their own, notably the Presbytery. This is a prolongation of the choir to the east without aisles, an arrangement which admits of large windows on each side which flood the extremity of the church with light. This feature, which we have already noticed in the romanesque abbeys, is only found in the largest of the First Pointed churches. More often the choir has no aisles. This aisleless choir is usually as high as the nave, and since there is no occasion for triforium or clerestory it assumes the form of a lofty hall lit by tall windows, which has no parallel in England except in the college chapels at Cambridge and Oxford. Its unusual character is emphasized when the windows are confined entirely or mainly to one side. This frequently happens in Scotland where it was the custom to build the sacristy or other buildings against the north wall, a very practical arrangement in a cold country. Choirs of this type with windows only to the south and east have a cheerful beauty of their own. The want of symmetry is readily accepted. The blank north walls must have offered a wonderful opportunity to the painter in fresco, though there is nothing left to show what use he made of it. The square form of the chapter house is another Scots feature. The use of the round arch long after it had been discarded in England has already been mentioned. These differences are mainly negative, but their cumulative effect is to give the Scots First Pointed churches a definitely national character.

We shall now make a brief survey of the older cathedrals, leaving to the next chapter the church of St. Giles, which only became a cathedral when the see of Edinburgh was created in the seventeenth century. The Norse cathedral of Kirkwall was described in the last chapter.

ST. ANDREWS CATHEDRAL (24) was the largest in the country as befitted the seat of the Archbishop and Primate. It was a splendid example of transitional work. Unfortunately it was so much destroyed at the Reformation and in the quarrying which followed, that the reader will find its ruins more interesting when he has mastered the design of other churches described below which remain comparatively intact. The conventual buildings at St. Andrews are of great interest, and thanks to the late Lord Bute have been well explored and the gatehouse repaired by the Office of Works. They show very clearly the fortifications and multifarious internal arrangements of a monastery of the first rank including gateway, barn, mill, dovecot and inn. Within the precincts is the ancient church of St. Rule or Regulus, with its lofty tower, built in the first half of the twelfth century. The building is well preserved. The chancel probably ended in an apse similar to those at Leuchars and Dalmeny. To the west of the tower, which is pierced by arches, there was a nave considerably wider than the tower itself judging by the scar of the roof. This building no doubt served as a cathedral before the foundation of its great successor was laid.

GLASGOW CATHEDRAL (25) is by far the most complete of the Scots cathedrals, and the only one which has never been roofless. But for the removal of the western towers—a sadly mistaken effort of the nineteenth century to get back to the thirteenth —the stone-work of the church would remain to-day almost exactly as successive generations of our forebears made it. The site, to which the High Street leads up from the Clyde, is hallowed by the memory of St. Mungo. Beyond it lies the little valley in which the Saint lived. It was here that St. Mungo was visited by St. Columba and pastoral staves exchanged as a token of friend-ship. The Molindinar burn, from which the Saint drew his water, has long been imprisoned in a pipe, but the valley remains, encumbered now with houses and overlooked by a crowded ceme-tery. The church may possibly enshrine the site of the Saint's cell as well as his tomb. Rising abruptly from the valley in surroundings so changed and sordid, its beautiful walls smothered in industrial dirt, this cathedral proclaims more clearly than any other the contrast between our restless mechanized existence of to-day and the simple faith and lovely craftsmanship of the Scot eight centuries ago.

Building was begun by Bishop Joceline in the last years of the twelfth century. Little, if any, of his work remains though the design was probably his. This design was loyally followed by succeeding generations, with so little regard for changes of fashion that it is difficult to realize that the work continued for more than two hundred years.

The steep slope to the east afforded an opportunity for under-building, of which good use was made by raising the choir on an under church or crypt. Bishop Bondington (1233-58) built most of the under church and choir. The crypt with its forest of pillars and beautiful vaulting is the most memorable part of the church. The alternation of large pillars supporting the piers of the choir with smaller pillars added for strength gives rise to a complicated and enchanting perspective, to which the unusual grouping of the inner pillars which carry the choir floor adds further complication and mystery. The central section of the inner vaulting is slightly later than the rest as may be seen from certain springers still visible and evidently intended for a simpler design. This happy afterthought included the site of St. Mungo's tomb, a low platform flanked by four slender shafts, very solemn in the dim light. Alas, not a trace of the shrine itself survives unless among fragments in the chapter house.

The chapter house, entered by a richly carved doorway at the north-east corner of the lower church, is of the same date. It is square after the Scots manner with vaulting supported on a central pillar and windows in all four walls. It seems to have been left unfinished in the thirteenth century and completed by Bishop Lauder early in the fifteenth, with the sacristy above it. The Dean's seat is a later insertion.

The choir naturally conforms in plan to the lower church, but is much more lofty. It has vaulted aisles and a triforium and clerestory, all of superb design. The ambulatory is carried across the east end of the church, an unusual but very attractive arrangement which must have been of great convenience for the services of the church and its processions. Beyond this eastern aisle are four chapels. Students of composition will be interested in the design of the east end.

It consists of twin arches opening into the aisle and above them a tall four-light window. The dual character of this arrangement in which the pier carrying the arches and mullion of the window form the actual centre may be open to criticism, but the designer no doubt counted on the altar and its canopy to pull his design together.

The nave is believed to have been built about 1300. It is one of the most important works carried out during the War of Independence, but is marred by the poor design and workmanship of the triforium and is perhaps the least interesting part of the church. The shafts which spring from the stringcourse above the main arcade have been taken as an indication that a vaulted roof was contemplated, but the necessary support is not provided.

The level of the nave floor lies half way between those of the lower church and choir, a very stately arrangement. The entrance to the choir is through a stone screen approached by a flight of steps, with stairs descending on each side to the crypt. The screen is of fifteenth-century work, rather coarse, but precious as the only thing of its kind left in Scotland, except those in the ruined churches of Melrose and Lincluden.

Before it stand two altar platforms with the arms of Bishop Blackadder who became bishop in 1484.

The furniture of the church has unfortunately completely disappeared. From a description which survives and the traces of the fastenings still evident in the stonework, the fittings appear to have been very elaborate, including, besides the stalls and screens enclosing the choir, a rood loft in the nave in front of Blackadder's screen and screens dividing the aisles of the nave into a series of chapels. The monuments in the church and churchyard are mostly of the sixteenth and seventeenth centuries. Those in the church include one of the few brasses remaining in Scotland.

It is greatly to the credit of Glasgow that the citizens have more than once risen to protect the cathedral when threatened with injury. Against the more insidious restorers of the nineteenth century they were unfortunately powerless. The building belongs to the Crown and is well cared for by H.M. Office of Works. A society of 'Friends of the Cathedral' has lately been formed and it is hoped that official care supplemented by private effort may in the near future restore to the church much of its lost beauty.

The bishop's castle, which was close to the cathedral, has completely disappeared. There seem never to have been any of the usual conventual buildings. It is known that the prebendaries, thirty-two in number, had separate manses. The only one remaining, PROVAND'S LORDSHIP (3), in Cathedral Square, is now the home of an antiquarian club and the scene of many happy gatherings and discussions. The country house of the same prebendary of Provand, about four miles east of the centre of the city, also survives. Through the good offices of the club, aided by other societies, it has recently been acquired for the National Trust and is at the moment of writing undergoing a careful restoration. It is vain to cry over spilt milk, but one can see now how easily the medieval character of the High Street and hill top might have been preserved without in any way impeding the development of the city.

Of all Scotland's ruined churches the Cathedral of Moray at ELGIN (26) is most to be regretted. When the see of Moray was transferred here from Spynie in 1224, the cathedral of the Holy Trinity was founded by Bishop Andrew de Moravia on the site of an earlier church with the same dedication. The history of the building is complicated by two fires, one in 1270 and the other the work of the Wolf of Badenoch, Earl of Buchan, in 1390, both of which are recorded to have destroyed it. In neither case can the destruction have been more than partial, though a good deal of rebuilding was required. The church is still essentially a work of the thirteenth century and shares with Glasgow Cathedral the honour of being one of the finest of that great period. All the component parts of a first class cathedral are found here. Two noble towers flank the west door, which is richly moulded : the nave has double aisles, now, alas, completely destroyed : at the crossing between the transepts the four great piers supported a central tower. The choir terminates in a presbytery lit by large windows and flanked by graceful turrets. There is no triforium, but the clerestory has an arcade with a passage between it and the windows. On the south a broad aisle served as a lady chapel : on the north an octagonal chapter house opened from a narrower aisle. The nave and chapter house seem to have suffered most in the fires, as they were largely reconstructed in the fifteenth century. The outer aisles of the nave were evidently an afterthought. They were restored in the fifteenth century, but appear to have been added as early as the thirteenth century, perhaps after the first fire.

This splendid pile was intact up to 1538 when the central tower showed signs of weakness and was rebuilt. Three years earlier Patrick Hepburn, son of the first Earl of Bothwell, had been made bishop. He sold much of the land from which the cathedral derived its resources and the ruin of the building dates from his time. It was the victim of greed and politics. In 1568 the lead was stripped from the roofs to provide pay for the army of the Regent Moray—to no purpose since the ship was sunk which carried it to Holland for sale. The roof remained unprotected till 1637, when a storm blew down the rafters. In 1640 the wooden screen between the nave and choir was torn down by authority of the General Assembly, with its precious paintings which are recorded by Spalding to have been in excellent preservation. The tracery of the great west window is believed to have been destroyed by Cromwell's troops between 1650 and 1660. In 1711 the central tower fell, completely crushing the nave. Then till 1807 the church became the quarry of the

ELGIN CATHEDRAL

26

DUNBLANE CATHEDRAL

27

district. The four great gables survive and part of the choir, all thirteenth-century work of outstanding beauty.

The chapter house, rebuilt after the fire on its old foundations, with a fine fifteenth-century vault resting on a central pillar, is nearly complete though most of its windows have lost their tracery. This form of chapter house, one of the loveliest products of Gothic building, is quite customary in England, but only two examples remain in Scotland, here and at Inchcolm. A stone reading desk forms part of the design of the central pillar.

There are remains of some fine tombs and several fragments of beautiful sculpture. The ruins have been put in excellent order since the church was taken over by H.M. Office of Works.

The four lower stories of the tower are the oldest part of DUNBLANE CATHEDRAL (27). If, as is generally believed, the tower was an eleventh-century addition to the church founded here by St. Blane, it forms a direct link with Columban times. The cathedral as it stands to-day is a fine work of the thirteenth century and nowhere did the First Pointed style produce a more beauti-

ful composition than in the west front. It is
very small and very simple compared with the
great façades of France and England, but it
would be difficult even in those countries to find
features so lovely in themselves combined in so
happy a proportion. The nave, with its noble
arcades and clerestory with double tracery, is also
of rare beauty. The lack of shafts linking the
main capitals with the roof may be a departure
from the Gothic tradition, but is very restful
and much to be preferred to the meaningless
vaulting shafts usually found in large English
churches where there are no groins to carry.
The choir is still more distinctly Scots—a great
hall brilliantly lit by windows on the south
and east, with the north wall blank except for
small windows high up and one tall window
beside the altar forming with its neighbour on the
south side a sort of presbytery. Behind the blank
wall is a long vaulted chamber known as the lady
chapel, but more probably the chapter house,
with scriptorium above.

For many years the nave stood roofless. The
choir, still used as a church, had undergone an
early nineteenth-century restoration. In 1889
the whole building was carefully restored by Sir

R. Rowand Anderson, who roofed the nave, re-placed the thirteenth-century tracery in the choir and pierced the blank wall to make room for a large organ. In 1912 Sir Robert Lorimer added stalls and a new reredos and organ case. The east window is filled with glass by C. E. Kempe. The other windows in the choir are the work of Mr. Louis Davis. Thus have four great ecclesi-astical artists laboured to restore the splendour of this ancient shrine.

So little furniture survived the Reformation in Scotland that Dunblane may be counted for-tunate in retaining six of its old canopied stalls. They appear to have been made for Bishop James Chisholm who reigned from 1486 to 1527. The carving is rich and full of spirit. Like all fine woodwork in Scotland it has been attributed to Flemish craftsmen, but there is no reason why it should not have been native work.

DUNKELD CATHEDRAL (28) owes its secluded site on a green meadow in the gorge of the Tay to the desire of the Pictish kings to place their mother church out of reach of the Norsemen who had made havoc of its predecessor in Iona. The relics of St. Columba or part of them were accordingly brought here from that island in 850.

The primacy of the Pictish Church was soon transferred to Abernethy, but the monastery remained and two centuries later the bishopric of Dunkeld was created by Alexander I in 1107.

Of the Pictish Church nothing remains and little of the thirteenth-century building which succeeded it, except a piece of fine arcading in the choir. For the architect the existing church has a special interest since one of its sixteenth-century canons, Alexander Mylne, afterwards Abbot of Cambuskenneth, has placed on record the dates of the various buildings. From this it appears that the choir was rebuilt by Bishop Sinclair, the friend of Robert the Bruce, who died in 1337. It is without aisles, and attached to its north wall is a rectangular chapter house, which now serves as the burial place of the Dukes of Atholl. This part of the church was much re-built in the early nineteenth century. The nave with its aisles was begun in 1406 by Bishop Cardeny whose monument is on the south wall. The date is interesting because the circular pillars would suggest an earlier period until the mouldings of the capitals and bases are examined. The large west window is a good example of the medieval disregard for symmetry : the staircase turret encroaches so much on the west wall that the window could not be placed in the centre of the gable. The tower, a particularly fine one, was added by Bishop Lauder later in the fifteenth century. Where the north aisle joins it there is a square-headed window with three lights. Windows of this type, familiar in Tudor buildings south of the Border, are seldom found in Scotland, but in Dunblane Cathedral and St. John's Church at Perth, there are similar windows in the same position. No explanation of this feature common to the three great Perthshire churches, so far as the writer knows, has yet been suggested. In the choir is the tomb of the Wolf of Badenoch, far too good for the destroyer of Elgin Cathedral.

In this church nothing is more to be regretted than the loss of the ancient glass. Bishop Cardeny had filled all the windows of the choir before his death in 1436, Bishop Lauder those of the nave between 1450 and 1481. Of this great collection not a fragment remains. When the church was purged at the Reformation in 1561 an order was made that the glass should be spared, but alas, it was destroyed along with all the other fittings.

Little is left of BRECHIN CATHEDRAL (8) except the west wall and the beautiful remains of the thirteenth-century choir which was perhaps never finished. The arcades of the old nave are included in the modern church, which has been widened and re-roofed. The west front may almost claim to be an epitome of building in Scotland. It is flanked on the right by the famous round tower which dates from about 1000; the transition doorway was built about 1200; the window above about a hundred years later. The tower on the left was begun about 1350; the spire after 1400; finally the aisle window brings us down to 1806, a period in all of no less than 800 years.

The ruins of the Cathedral of Ross are at FORT-ROSE in the Black Isle, near the shore of the Moray Firth. The first seat of the Bishop of Ross was at Rosemarkie, about a mile further east than the ruined church which we are now considering. At Rosemarkie there was a Culdee college which David I seems to have converted into a cathedral chapter, the head of the college being appointed bishop. The transfer of the cathedral was probably made about 1235 when the chapter was enlarged by absorbing a chanonry which occupied the new site. By a charter of James II the two places were united under the name of

28 Above: DUNKELD CATHEDRAL
Below: WHITHORN PRIORY, from a drawing by Sir Herbert Maxwell

ABERDEEN CATHEDRAL

ABERDEEN CATHEDRAL

Fortrose. Nothing remains to-day of the thir-teenth-century church unless it be the crypt below the chapter house. The nave and choir have completely disappeared. The vaulted aisle which survives is a beautiful work of the four-teenth century. It appears to have been an addition, since it has a separate roof of its own with gables at each end, instead of the usual lean-to arrangement. The eastern section is wider than the western and the point where the two meet is marked by a picturesque turret containing a stair which led to rooms above the vault.

There are remains of two fine monuments, a very charming piscina and a font. All the tracery of the windows has unfortunately been broken. What is left of the building has been put in good order by H.M. Office of Works and the founda-tions of the vanished church have been exposed.

This church had much the same fate as Elgin Cathedral. The lead was stripped from the roof under the Regent Morton, but the building re-mained in fairly good condition until the middle of the seventeenth century. It then became a quarry, being used, it is believed, by Cromwell for the construction of the fortress at Inverness.

St. Machar's Cathedral (29) at Old Aber-

DEEN is one more of David I's foundations, but the building itself is less ancient than most of those we have been considering and only the nave remains of a much larger church. Of First Pointed work nothing is left, but the pillars of red freestone at the east end of the existing building date from about 1370. With two other piers, now destroyed, they carried the tower which crowned the crossing. The rest of the existing church is of granite, except the spires which are of a grey freestone. The granite work was built between 1422 and 1440 and never has this intractable material been used to better purpose. The west front with its low doorway and seven-light window, flanked by the low, almost windowless towers with corbelled parapets like the castles of the day, seems the very embodiment of massive strength, contemptuous of ornament, but thanks to its fine proportions by no means devoid of beauty.

The spires of the squat type which we shall see later was characteristic of Scots work, were added in the sixteenth century. They are in perfect harmony with the towers and help to make this relatively small building one of the most impressive in the world. The porch with its crow stepped gables and upper room seems to be an echo of the porch at Linlithgow. The nave with its round pillars and wide aisles is very spacious. The oak ceiling of the church is the work of Bishop Dunbar, who also built the spires. It was designed by 'James Winter, an Angus man' and is decorated with the armorial bearings of European potentates, including Pope Leo X and those of certain Scots worthies of the sixteenth century. There are three fine monuments, those of Bishop Dunbar and Bishop Scougal and a very curious miniature recumbent effigy in low relief supposed to represent Archdeacon Barbour, the poet.

Dornoch Cathedral stands in the centre of the charming town which shares with Clackmannan the distinction of being the smallest county town in Scotland. Across the road stands the tower of the Bishop's Castle. St. Gilbert, who was consecrated Bishop of Caithness in 1223, was the founder of this church and probably its architect. He was a member of the great family of Moravia (or Murray), whose work we shall see at Bothwell and was himself the builder of the great fortress of Kildrummy. The church as it now stands is a large cruciform building without aisles. The nave is quite modern. It replaces a nave with aisles which was long in ruins. The modern walls have been cut away beside the western piers of the crossing to show the spring of the old arcades. The choir and transepts have three large lancet windows in each gable and windows of the same type in pairs in the side walls. A slight projection supported on small arches and corbels runs all round this part of the church forming a sort of machicolated frieze above the windows. In the spaces between the windows it drops to a lower level, thus dividing the walls into a series of well-defined bays to which the design of the plaster roof lends further emphasis. On the outside the windows have wide rather flat mouldings of a form which might pass for First Pointed. How far this is the original building and how far a seventeenth-century reconstruction it is difficult to say, but the masonry does not resemble that of the thirteenth century. The building as it stands is simple and impressive both inside and out. The inside has lately been stripped of its plaster and though the rubble masonry was certainly not intended to be seen, the effect is harmonious and dignified. It is much enhanced by a number of good modern windows. This church seems to have escaped the notice of MacGibbon and Ross though the Bishop's Castle, which stands just across the street, is noticed by them. The tower of this building, once used as a Tolbooth but now incorporated in a modern house, appears to be mainly of the sixteenth century. A massive chimney, known as the Bishop's chimney, may be part of an older building.

For convenience a note on IONA CATHEDRAL (10) is included here, though very little of the existing building is older than the fifteenth century and it was not till 1507 that it became the Cathedral of the Isles. The reader need not be reminded that Icolmkil has been a place of pilgrimage for Scotsmen ever since St. Columba landed there more than thirteen centuries ago. The cathedral is by no means the most ancient of its buildings. The adjoining church of St. Ronan and the chapel of St. Oran are both older. They are well worth a visit if only for their wealth of sculptured stones, as also is the Nunnery with its thirteenth century church and interesting conventual buildings.

The Columban monastery founded in 563 was a short distance north of the cathedral, where traces of it may still be seen. It was transferred to the present site in 818 after destruction by the Norsemen. The new buildings met the same fate in a subsequent raid and appear to have remained in ruins while the Norsemen had possession of the isles. In 1156 the islands south of Ardnamurchan were surrendered to Somerled, King of Argyll. Monks of the Benedictine order were introduced by his son Reginald about 1203 and a nunnery of the same order was also founded. The deed of confirmation of that date is still preserved in the Vatican.

The cathedral is the most ambitious building on the island, and with its monastic adjuncts belongs to the late fifteenth and early sixteenth centuries. Only two small chapels on the east side of the north transept seem to have belonged to an earlier church. The chief architectural interest lies here, as elsewhere in the West Highlands, in the persistence of Celtic design in the relatively late period to which most of these buildings belong. It is used effectively on the capitals as well as on the crosses and sepulchral monuments. The architecture is crude as might be expected in so remote a place, but not careless or clumsy. Some of the details are indeed very beautiful, not least the window tracery which is of a type which goes admirably with the granite walls. The low arched buttresses on which the aisle roof rests are at first sight a puzzling feature. They were dictated by the unusual position of the clerestory windows—over the pillars instead of over the arches—which made it necessary to keep the buttresses below the sill of the windows. The church, long a ruin, has been re-roofed. It is used for divine service, and is once more a place of pilgrimage. The sculptural stones are well cared for.

Enough remains of the cloister and abbey buildings to show their scale and arrangement. They are on the north side of the church, an unusual position dictated in this case by the exigencies of the water supply. In the building at the extreme end of the eastern range the channel may still be seen which conducted a stream of water through the monastic drain.

The Priory Church of WHITHORN (28) served as the CATHEDRAL OF GALLOWAY. We have seen that nothing remains of St. Ninian's Candida Casa except the name which persists, in formal documents at least, till the Reformation. The oldest part of the existing priory dates from its founda-

tion by Fergus, Lord of Galloway in 1124. The
fine Romanesque door is of that date though it
shows traces of having been rebuilt. The church
to which it belonged was probably quite small.
In the thirteenth or fourteenth century it was
widened to the north and a new choir and western
tower were added. This church was a favourite
place of pilgrimage and many Scots sovereigns,
beginning with Kenneth II in 970 and ending
with Mary Queen of Scots, came to worship at the
shrine of St. Ninian. Pious offerings enriched
the priory and the cathedral church was greatly
enlarged in the fifteenth century. The old church
became the nave of the new and to the east transepts and choir on a larger scale were added.

Of all this splendour little now remains except
part of the south wall of the old church and the
eastern extremity of the fifteenth century choir.
The east end with its dual arrangement seems to
have been copied from Glasgow Cathedral.

We cannot close this chapter without mention-
ing three important monasteries which belong to
the earlier part of the period, the Abbeys of Holyrood and Arbroath and the Priory of Pluscarden.

The church of ARBROATH ABBEY (30) was of
great size and the surviving remnants show that

30 Above:
PLUSCARDEN
PRIORY

Below:
ARBROATH
ABBEY

ABBEY OF HOLYROOD

the design was exceptionally massive. It is difficult to imagine anything more straightforward or bolder than the gable of the south transept. The simple mouldings and arcades which are its only adornment are used with great skill to emphasize its scale. The remnants of the abbot's house and other monastic buildings are of special interest.

PLUSCARDEN PRIORY (11, 30) was founded by Alexander II in 1236 for monks of the Order of Valliscaulium who also had houses in the Highlands at Beauly and Ardchattan. Of the thirteenth-century buildings only the choir and transepts of the church remain, with the tower over the crossing, and the sacristy and part of the chapter house. Large circular windows are conspicuous features in the transepts. The south transept is remarkable for its ingenious combination of clerestory and triforium. The choir, of which the date is undetermined, built early in the fifteenth century, was intended to be a daring structure with very large windows and a vaulted roof, of which the springers still remain. The design was so faulty that the stone roof was not attempted. The windows were reduced in size when the original Order, under whom the monastery had languished, was superseded by the Benedictines in

1460. The nave was never completed. The eastern range of conventual buildings survives, but was much altered by a former owner, Lord Fife. Careful repairs and interesting excavations have been made since the priory was acquired by the late Lord Bute.

The ABBEY CHURCH OF HOLYROOD (31) is far more elaborate. This was one of the few completely vaulted buildings in Scotland. Its beautiful detail claims careful study from any student who wishes to learn the right way of applying ornament. Holyrood was one of David I's foundations and always a favourite residence of the Scots kings. The magnificent church seems to have remained fairly intact till the middle of the sixteenth century, when it was twice raided and burnt by the English. Before the end of the century the choir and transepts had completely disappeared but the nave survived and was used as the Chapel Royal. It was restored for this purpose by Charles I and James VII, while still Duke of York, with stalls for the Knights of the Thistle. These fittings were destroyed by the mob in 1688, but the east and west windows of the Caroline period survive. The ruin of the nave did not occur till the middle of the seventeenth century, when the old walls collapsed under the weight of a new stone roof. Lord Leven, a Knight of the Thistle and more than once High Commissioner to the Church of Scotland, who died in 1906, left a provisional bequest for the restoration of the Chapel Royal. Under Lord Leven's will Lord Crawford and the writer were appointed to decide whether the project should be carried out. They sought the advice of the late Professor Lethaby. He considered the building unsuitable for restoration on the ground that its frailty would necessitate a reconstruction so complete as to destroy its value as an authentic document. The First Commissioner of Works, whose consent was necessary, shared this view. This decision caused great disappointment at the time, especially to Lord Rosebery, the most distinguished of living Scotsmen, who regarded it as a pedantic sacrifice of an historic opportunity to architectural technique. Lord Leven's family, to whom the money reverted, generously found another way to carry out his wish by building the Thistle Chapel attached to St. Giles'. Thus the broken arches of the old abbey remain undisturbed, while a new building of exceptional beauty has come into existence.

This tale of First Pointed buildings is by no means complete. Among buildings which have not been mentioned the Abbey of Kilwinning and Priory of Beauly, though much ruined, are both well worth a visit. Those which will probably attract the reader most, on account of their romantic situation and the vivid picture they give of religious life in the Middle Ages, are two small island monasteries, the Abbey of Inchcolm in the Firth of Forth and the Priory of INCHMAHOME (32) in the Lake of Menteith. He would do well to devote a summer afternoon to each of these and examine the buildings at leisure with the excellent little guide books provided by H.M. Office of Works. Nor ought the Abbeys of CROSSRAGUEL in Ayrshire or LUCE (41) in Galloway to be missed. Little early work remains in either, but the later buildings are of great interest and all the old foundations have been exposed.

Parish churches of this period are few, but remains of First Pointed work will be found at Prestonkirk and Pencaitland in East Lothian. The ruined church of Lanark is a finer example, as are also the chapels of DUNSTAFFNAGE (59) and Skipness in Argyll.

CHAPTER V

MIDDLE POINTED PERIOD—THE LATER ABBEYS
1286–1460

The death of Alexander III in 1286 marked the end of Scotland's great church building era. The century which followed was disturbed by rival claims to the crown, by the interference of Edward I and his successors in the affairs of Scotland and the determined and successful effort of the Scots to retain their independence. Such events did not encourage building. We shall see in a later chapter how lay efforts in that line underwent a marked shrinkage both in numbers and scale. The Church was rich and there was no lack of good masons. Some notable ecclesiastical building was done. It shows in most cases no falling off in quality. But there were fewer new foundations and many of the old monasteries were sacked and burnt in the ruthless forays which swept over Scotland from the south during these stormy years. Those in the border country naturally suffered most.

Church building in Scotland had hitherto followed English models, and though later in date, and as we have seen deficient in certain features, was not inferior in craftsmanship. In the period we are now considering the lag in date increased and the differences became so marked that the Scots churches began to assume a definitely national character. Architecturally the limits of this period are not very clearly defined. Even in England it is impossible to draw a sharp line between the first and second pointed styles. One merges into the other. But in England the change, though gradual, is very apparent. Severity gives place to exuberance. Windows become larger. Tracery becomes more elaborate. Cusping is added. Mouldings become richer. Carved ornaments develop from conventional forms into lovely renderings of real flowers and leaves. The ribs of the vaulting are multiplied and their intersections adorned with numerous bosses. Sculptured figures assume new grace and life. In our simpler Scots buildings similar changes occur, but they are less evident.

The end of the period is no more sharply defined in Scotland than the beginning. The date assigned to it—1460—is not a political date. It

INCHMAHOME PRIORY

MELROSE ABBEY

33

merely marks the completion of work at Melrose and elsewhere in the Middle Pointed or Decorated style.

At MELROSE ABBEY (33) the decorated style is seen at its best. This abbey was founded by David I near the site of an earlier monastery, but the buildings seem to have been completely destroyed by Edward II when he invaded Scotland in 1322. The church was rebuilt with money provided by Robert the Bruce. It was burnt or partially burnt by Richard II in 1385. Important additions were made by Abbot Hunter about the middle of the fifteenth century. Its glory was finally destroyed by the English under Hertford in 1545. The church consists of a long nave, intended to be longer, transepts and an unusually short choir, so short that three bays of the nave were included in the space allotted to the monks. The east end terminates in a square presbytery. With the exception of the Abbey Church of Holyrood this is the only large church in Scotland which was vaulted throughout. The narrowness of the north aisle, which contrasts sharply with the spaciousness of the rest of the building, is explained by the fact that an older cloister prevented expansion in that direction. The main arcade of the nave and one surviving wall of the central tower are the only parts which can be ascribed to Bruce's benefaction. The choir, transepts and south aisle of the nave with its chapels appear to have been built after the fire of 1385 and form the finest and most elaborate example of 'decorated' work in Scotland. They bear a strong resemblance to the nave of York Minster which was built about 1400. The flying buttresses which support the vaults are the best example of that device north of the Tweed. Some of the pinnacles with their recessed niches and panelling are very like English work. Others, after the Scots manner, have figures standing on brackets and under canopies, but against plain stone work without niches. The tracery of some of the windows is almost 'perpendicular'. Others are designed with the flamboyant curves which later became popular in Scotland. The large window of the south transept is a perfect example of 'decorated' tracery. The church is full of delicate carving wrought in a lovely red sandstone which has retained its sharpness and is of rare beauty. A few niches retain their figures, but they are not of such fine quality. The barrel roof which dominates the nave survives from an attempt to restore that part of the church for parochial use in 1618.

At Melrose we have seen a splendour unusual in Scots churches. At SWEETHEART ABBEY (34) on the Solway Firth we find a smaller, simpler and earlier building which is far more typical of Scots work. The plan (p. 24) has all the national characteristics. The choir is short and aisleless. The transepts have aisles only on the east. These and the aisles of the nave are the only parts of the building which have been vaulted. The tower is crowned by a saddle roof surrounded by a parapet—just like the castles of the day. The round arch persists in the minor doors and windows. There is no triforium, but in front of the clerestory windows there are triple arches opening into the church. These arches are the most charming features of the building. In 1779 the ruins had a narrow escape. They were sold as a quarry, but bought back by the indignant neighbours, subject to the mason's right to any stones which fell. It would be difficult in any country to find a more attractive ruin. The walls of rose-coloured sandstone rise from green lawns. It was a happy idea of one of the late owners, Mr. Richard Oswald of Auchincruive, to create these lawns. His work has been maintained by the Office of Works, in whose charge the building now is, and his example followed at other places in their custody. The windows frame exquisite landscapes. The site, sheltered from the north by Criffel and looking across the Solway to the Cumberland Hills is famous for its fine oaks and limes and lofty pines. Criticism in such a scene seems like sacrilege. But if the architecture is coldly examined it will be seen that it lacks not only the splendour of Melrose but also its fine design and craftsmanship. The pointed arches are awkwardly depressed—that is, the curves are drawn from a centre below the spring. The tracery of two of the principal windows seems to have given way, for they have been replaced by smaller windows and solid masonry. But nowhere else can the peculiar merits and faults of Scots 'decorated' work be better studied. The foundress, Devorgilla, was the wife of John Balliol. Balliol College at Oxford owes its foundation to her, and she built the first bridge over the Nith at Dumfries. She founded the abbey in memory of her husband and when she died in 1289 his heart, which she had carried about with her in an ivory box, was buried beside her in front of the high altar. Thence the

SWEETHEART ABBEY

35   LINCLUDEN COLLEGE

name, Dulce Cor. It was also known as New Abbey to distinguish it from the older abbey of Dundrennan. Melrose, Dundrennan and Sweetheart all belonged to the Cistercian Order.

LINCLUDEN COLLEGE (35) near Dumfries, but in the county of Kirkcudbright, was founded about 1400 by Archibald the Grim, Earl of Douglas, on the site of a nunnery which he suppressed. The monument to his son's widow, sister of King James I, is built into the wall of the choir. She died about 1440. The work is therefore probably of the same date as that at Melrose. It has the same excellence. Only the church and scanty remnants of the college survive. The church consists of a short nave with an aisle and transept on the south side and a well lit choir of three bays. The tracery of the windows is broken, but enough remains to show that it was of the geometric type found in the best buildings of the period, like the large window of the south transept at Melrose. A stone screen divides the choir from the nave. The church was vaulted throughout. Above the groined vaulting there was a plain barrel vault carrying the stone roof. The same arrangement is found in St. Mirin's Chapel at Paisley Abbey. This must be one of the earliest collegiate churches. The establishment here consisted of a Provost and twelve canons who lived in buildings attached to the church. A collegiate church on these lines cannot have been very different from a small abbey or priory, except that it required no papal bull.

The chapter house at Elgin and the one remaining aisle of Fortrose are admirable works of this period which have already been mentioned. The Parish Church of Haddington, the nave of the Church of Stirling and the chapter house of Balmerino Abbey in Fife, though designed with less delicacy, are also important examples.

The most complete and best preserved large parish church of this period is that of St. Michael's at Linlithgow (43). In style and plan it stands halfway between the 'decorated' type and that evolved in Scotland during the succeeding period. The nave and choir with their aisles form one long hall uninterrupted by the usual crossing. In place of transepts there are two chapels, which, like the porches, are separate buildings attached to the church, but each with its own roof and gables. It was in the south transept, while he was praying at the altar of St. Katherine, that James IV saw his vision of a bald man clad in a blue gown who foretold his defeat and death at Flodden. The aisles have ribbed vaults. The main alley, which has an oak roof, terminates at the east end in an apse and at the west in a tower. The whole seems to have been built after a fire which destroyed the older church in 1424. The nave is older than the choir and tower and closer to the 'decorated' ideal, as will be seen from the capitals which are moulded to the shape of the shafts and arches, whereas those of the other parts of the church take the form of straight bands. The apse, one of the earliest of its kind in Scotland, is attached to the east wall like a large bow window. The transept chapels and porches have rooms above them and with their stair turrets and stepped gables are beautiful examples of Scots design. The south porch has a neat oriel above the door similar to one in the adjoining palace and another of later date in the castle of Maybole. This is a rare feature in Scotland. The tower was originally finished with an open crown like that at St. Giles'. This became insecure and was removed early in the last century. Without it the tower looks gaunt and meaningless like an empty pedestal. The restoration of the crown top is much to be desired. If there is doubt about the ability of the tower to carry the weight it should be possible with modern appliances to reinforce it or if necessary rebuild it. The church and palace together form one of the finest architectural groups in this country, but their unity is sadly impaired by the lack of this dominating feature.

Of great interest are three smaller churches, St. Monan's in Fife, and the Lanarkshire churches of Bothwell and Douglas, both dedicated to St. Bride.

St. Monan's Church (36) stands bravely facing the east wind on the rocky coast near Anstruther. Its date is rather a puzzle. The Exchequer Rolls show that a church was erected here for David II between 1362 and 1370 at a cost of £620, but nothing in the church, except perhaps the groined vault, resembles work of that period. On the other hand the whole building corresponds to work of the middle of the fifteenth century. We can only assume that David II's church must have been rebuilt. The present church consists of a chancel of four bays with transepts and a tower over the crossings. There is no nave. The east end has two windows with a buttress between them, an arrangement which

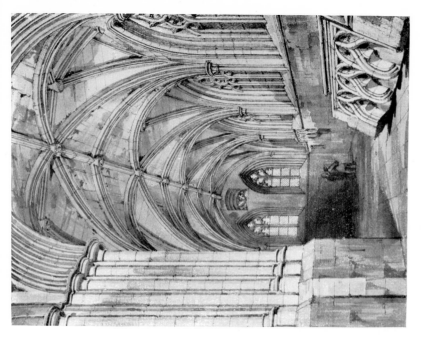

ST. MONAN'S

ST. MONAN'S

ST. BRIDE'S,
DOUGLAS

ST. BRIDE'S,
BOTHWELL

37

is very attractive in a small church. The east
windows are narrower than the others, but they
are all of the same height. A small horizontal
window over the central buttress has a segmental
top which picks up the outer curves of the twin
windows below it.

Of ST. BRIDE'S CHURCH at DOUGLAS (37) only
the choir and bell turret remain. It is remarkable for three fine monuments with recumbent
figures, which commemorate the good Sir James
and the fifth and seventh Earls of Douglas. These
are all of the fifteenth century and the two first
are of rare beauty. The figure of the good Sir
James may be a century older than the canopy.
A rather florid recumbent alabaster figure by
Boehm of Lady Home, heiress of Douglas, will
interest students of nineteenth-century sculpture.

Of the COLLEGIATE CHURCH OF ST. BRIDE at
BOTHWELL (37) again only the chancel remains.
It was founded by Archibald the Grim, Earl of
Douglas, in 1393. The roof is an early example
of a barrel vault decorated with ribs. The side
windows are kept below the spring of the vault
which makes the church darker and less attractive
than St. Monan's, and the large arch of the east
window is depressed and squat, its curves havin.

been drawn from a centre well below the level from which they spring. The church has pre-served its old flagged roof, an excellent example of this characteristically Scots construction. At-tached to the old chancel, but without access to it, there was a large modern church. Recently this church has undergone a drastic reconstruc-tion and has been united to the old chancel. This work has been carried out with commendable frankness, but with such nice judgment that the combination of a spacious modern church with the ancient sanctuary seems as natural as it is happy. Attached to the north side of the chancel is the ancient sacristy, which has also retained its old slab roof.

St. Giles' Church (38), standing on the only level spot in the long ascent from Holyrood to the Castle, was the first parish church of Edin-burgh. Of its early history nothing is known except that a new church was built about 1120 of which scarcely anything remains. It was rebuilt again in the fourteenth century. There is no record of this, but five bays of the nave resemble other Scots work of this date and must have sur-vived the burning of the church by Richard II in 1385, since the two chapels to the south of it,

which still exist, were added in 1387 in the course
of the restoration which followed the fire. These
chapels, after the Reformation, were thrown into
one and now form an additional aisle parallel with
the nave. The church as completed in 1387
remains to this day though several important
additions have been made to it. On the north
side of the nave a porch leading into the middle
bay is the only surviving feature of the twelfth-
century church. To the west of this porch a
chapel, now known as the Albany Aisle, was
added soon after 1400. The capital of its central
pillar bears two shields with the arms of Robert,
Duke of Albany, and Archibald, Earl of Douglas.
These men were both implicated in the starving
to death of the Duke of Rothesay at Falkland
Palace in 1402 and it has been suggested that they
erected this chapel in expiation of their crime.
About the same period two other chapels were
added to the east of the Norman porch and probably the vault of the north aisle of the nave had
to be rebuilt when the outside wall was removed
to provide access to the new chapels.

The next series of changes were made in the
latter half of the fifteenth century. The choir
was lengthened by one bay and heightened to

admit of taller windows in the clerestory. The new vaulting is much more elegant than the old as will be seen by comparing it with the older vaulting in the aisles. The two new pillars of the additional bay and the responds on the east wall are adorned by an interesting and very beautiful display of heraldry. The north pillar, known as the King's pillar, bears the arms of James II facing west ; of his son who became James III facing east ; of Mary of Gueldres facing north ; and the Fleur de Lys of France facing south. As the young prince was not born till 1453 and his father was killed at the siege of Roxburgh in 1460 the building must have been done between these dates since the label on the prince's shield indicates that his father was still alive. On the other pillar the shield facing east bears the arms of William Preston of Gorton who bequeathed to the church an arm-bone of St. Giles which he had obtained from France at great expense ; that facing west bears the arms of Bishop Kennedy, grandson of Robert III and Bishop of St. Andrews ; that facing north the arms of Nicholas de Otterburn, Vicar of Edinburgh in 1455, and that facing south the arms of Edinburgh. The north respond bears the arms of Thomas Crans-

ST. GILES', EDINBURGH, INTERIOR

39   **ST. GILES', EDINBURGH**
Crown Steeple

ton, chief magistrate of Edinburgh in 1439 and again in 1454; the south respond those of Napier of Merchiston, Provost of Edinburgh in 1457. About this time another large chapel—the Preston Aisle—was added to the south of the choir to celebrate Sir William Preston's pious bequest of Saint Giles' arm. Part of the south wall was removed and replaced by three arches opening into the new chapel. It is here that the King's seat is placed. At this time both transepts were extended to suit the increased width of the church.

In the sixteenth century the width of the church was further increased by the addition of two more chapels—Lauder's Aisle, built by Alexander Lauder of Blyth, Provost of Edinburgh in 1513, which filled the space between the south transept and the south porch of the nave, and Chepman's Aisle, which was on the other side of the south transept. Walter Chepman had in 1507 introduced the art of printing into Scotland. James IV and Queen Margaret had helped him in this enterprise and he dedicated this chapel to the welfare of their souls. The dedication took place in August 1513, only nineteen days before the king was killed at Flodden.

St. Giles' suffered a good deal during the Reformation. The altars and images and famous relics were all destroyed in 1556. In 1560 it again became the parish church with John Knox as minister and was divided to accommodate two congregations, the High Church in the choir and Tolbooth Church in the nave. Other parts of the church served various secular purposes, such as schools, courts of justice and the town clerk's office, and a place was reserved for the 'Maiden', the instrument then used for the execution of criminals.

In 1633 Laud accompanied Charles I to Scotland for the coronation and, in the course of their famous attempt to foist Episcopacy on the country, St. Giles' became a cathedral. In 1637 it once more became Presbyterian and has remained so ever since except for a short break between 1661 and 1688, during which Episcopacy was restored.

For the next fifty years the church continued to be divided to serve all kinds of purposes. In 1829 the surrounding houses and booths with which it had become encumbered were removed and the exterior of the building went through a drastic renovation which completely obliterated the ancient character of both walls and windows. The only old window remaining is in the east wall of the north transept. Fortunately the central tower with its crown steeple escaped this cruel treatment.

There is no record of the date when the steeple (39) was built but it was probably erected about 1500, when the changes in the interior had been completed and the church had become 'collegiate'.* The only other surviving crown steeples in Scotland are those of King's College Chapel, Old Aberdeen, and the Tolbooth Steeple of Glasgow. In both the central feature—a cupola —is carried on four arched supports springing from the corners of the tower. At St. Giles' there are four additional supports springing from the centre of each side—a much more satisfying composition. Here the central feature is a lofty pinnacle surrounded by a pinnacled gallery. There were crowned steeples on the churches of Linlithgow and Haddington, but neither survives. The only other in Great Britain is at Newcastle on the church of St. Nicholas. This is older than any of the Scots examples. It is a

---

* The college at St. Giles' consisted of a provost, curate, sixteen prebendaries, a minister of the choir, four choristers, a sacristan, a beadle and numerous chaplains and other clergy, all supported out of its endowments.

graceful thing, but less massive and less interesting than those we have been considering.

The Thistle Chapel (40), of which the origin has been explained above, is the latest addition. It is the work of Sir Robert Lorimer and is generally reckoned his masterpiece. It may well be so. He flung himself into this undertaking as he never did into any other except perhaps the Scots National War Memorial.

The building is very small, measuring inside less than forty feet in length and twenty in width, but it is over forty feet high. Height was so essential to his design that he added an extra five feet to the walls while the work was in progress. Seldom has so small a space been rendered so impressive. In both stone and wood the design follows Scots fifteenth-century ideals, but it goes much further than the fifteenth-century artist ever had a chance of going. Within the ample sum set aside for the work the architect had a perfectly free hand. He chose craftsmen whom he could trust and gave them in turn, within the limits of the design and scale, free play for their imaginations and chisels in the carved work of the vault and stalls. The extreme elaboration of these parts is made more precious by plain walls and a

THISTLE CHAPEL

41   Above: CROSSRAGUEL ABBEY, ENTRANCE GATEWAY
Below: LUCE ABBEY, DOOR OF CHAPTER HOUSE

quiet treatment of the floor, also by the small scale of the building, which is little more than a casket. The only part of the design which appears open to question is the treatment of the panelling on each side of the King's Installation Chair. It introduces a domestic note foreign to the rest. But it is rash to criticize where every detail has been so carefully thought out, and Lorimer no doubt had good reason for this treatment. A telling contrast is supplied by the low vault of the ante-chapel. Here the choir is stationed during the brief service which is held every year on the Sunday next to St. Andrew's Day. In the chapel itself there is only room for the Dean, the Knights and the Heralds. This year when the King attended a chapter and the Queen was, by his command, installed a Lady of the Thistle, along with two new knights, it required good stage management on the part of the Dean to secure the smooth working of this impressive ceremony.

St. Giles' has been described at length because to Scotsmen it is perhaps the most interesting of all churches. Though small in scale and the work of many periods, its interior is one of the most impressive in the world. The various changes we have followed have brought this church to a shape most unusual in this country. On plan it is nearly square. There are four main alleys running east to west with chapels beyond them and these afford vistas of extraordinary variety and complexity. The crossing below the central tower, left at its original level when choir and nave were raised, adds a mysterious gloom to the centre of the church which is enhanced by the shadowy vaults of the windowless aisles. Here is harmony without uniformity. The rugged stonework, though not intended by its builders to be exposed, is beautiful in colour and texture. The building is full of monuments and associations with history. In the changed life of to-day it still holds its own as the place of worship of a large congregation and the scene of those solemn services which mark the life of a nation.

DUNGLASS COLLEGIATE CHURCH

43   Above: ST. MICHAEL'S, LINLITHGOW
      Below: ST. SALVATOR'S, ST. ANDREWS

CHAPTER VI

THIRD POINTED PERIOD—THE COLLEGIATE CHURCHES
1460–1700

This period extends from the date when the Middle Pointed or Decorated style was superseded by one more distinctly national, to the time when Gothic building was finally abandoned. Its early years saw the rebuilding of three cathedrals, Dunkeld, Iona and Aberdeen, which have already been described, and one important abbey church, that of Paisley. The large parish churches of Dundee, Perth and Stirling were also rebuilt at this time.

In England the transition from Middle to Third Pointed, from Decorated to Perpendicular, was accompanied by the introduction of new features which make it unmistakable. Such are the four centred arch, the square headed window, a new type of tracery, the panelling of walls, fan vaulting. In Scotland these features are unknown except in one or two buildings obviously copied from English models. In their absence the earlier forms continued in use and there is little to indicate the transition to late Gothic except a difference in scale and purpose when the Collegiate Church came into fashion and an increasing tendency to import castellated forms into ecclesiastical buildings.

Most of the new foundations were collegiate churches, built and endowed by pious individuals, the college consisting of the priests and choristers who conducted the services. Altogether forty of these churches were founded. A list is given in Appendix IV. A few, as we have seen at Lincluden, were on the site of earlier monastic houses, but most of them were new. Many are still in use. They were for the most part small and the builders seem to have had less experience than those who worked in the 'decorated' style in the preceding period. They were, for instance, very shy of ribbed vaults. The few on which they ventured are on a small scale. For wider spans they followed the example set at St. Bride's, Bothwell, and barrel vaults carrying slab roofs became the usual covering for both church and castle. The same builders were no doubt employed on both. For details of

TORPHICHEN CHURCH

From South-East

44

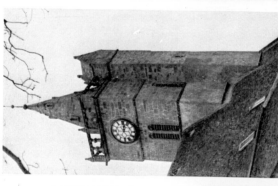

DAIRSIE

FIFE BELL TOWERS
ANSTRUTHER EASTER

CUPAR

45

towers, staircases, parapets and gables the church. borrowed freely from the castle. There was still a preference for the round arch, especially for doorways. Spires—unlike the soaring structures raised in the low countries and England at this time—were short and squat, though well proportioned to their solid towers. The towers themselves seldom had buttresses unless they were required to support a vaulted roof as in the fine tower of the Parish Church at Dundee. In the tracery of windows some flamboyant forms were still popular and the apse was of French origin. This feature, hitherto tacked on as we have seen at Linlithgow, became, in the smaller churches, an integral part of the building. Otherwise there was no resemblance to the buildings of France, still less to those of England where classical motives were beginning to modify and supersede the last phase of Gothic.

At no other time was church building in Scotland so distinctly national. The infusion of castellated forms contributed to this. The style excelled in picturesque effects rather than in grandeur or beauty. Avoidance of intersecting vaults put the finer achievements of Gothic beyond the builder's reach. Except in rare cases—

Rosslyn was one and Crail another—aisles were abandoned. If there was a central tower the crossing was usually kept low to allow the barrel vaults of the four arms to abut against solid walls. This was the case even at Seton where the crossing has a ribbed vault. In the absence of a central tower, as at Ladykirk, the barrel vault extended the full length of nave and chancel, but the windows and entrances to the transepts had to be kept below its spring which made the vault itself gloomy. Yet these simple interiors have great dignity and at their best real beauty, as well as a charming homeliness. Seen from outside, the design is completely dominated by the roof. Nothing could be more satisfactory. The permanency of a stone roof supported by a stone vault appeals to the mind as peculiarly suitable for a place of worship, while the eye delights in the fine workmanship and complicated perspective of the slabs alternately rounded and hollowed to drain off the rain.

The nave and transepts of PAISLEY ABBEY (46) were built about 1450 and the long aisleless choir, judging from the sedilia, must have been of the same period. In the lower part of the western front and in the north-east corner of the cloister parts of an earlier thirteenth-century church are incorporated. The interior of the nave is marred by a clumsy contrivance at the clerestory level which provides a gangway round sections of the wall which are not pierced by the usual passage. A distinguished architect with whom the writer happened to visit the Abbey made the interesting suggestion that these ungainly projections may be an afterthought. This view gains support from the fact that the corbels below them, from which the wall shafts were presumably intended to spring, are delicately carved and quite out of keeping with the coarse work above. The transepts and choir, roofless since the collapse of the central tower, have been restored in recent years by Paisley's generous sons and daughters. In 1898 the transepts and crossing were taken in hand by Sir R. Rowand Anderson, who also built the first stage of the central tower. In 1912 Dr. Macgregor Chalmers erected the walls of the choir on the old foundations and rebuilt part of the cloister. His design for the latter was based on the corbels which had survived the old cloister and on the discovery of one or more of the twin caps. In 1923, when the work was resumed after the war, Sir Robert

Lorimer added the groined roof of the choir and upper stage of the tower. Rowand Anderson had intended to carry the tower a good deal higher and finish it with a saddle roof, like that of the tower of Dundee, but steeper. Dr. Macgregor Chalmers, no doubt fearing the weight, abandoned this bold design in favour of a lower tower with a short spire in the Scots manner. Sir Robert Lorimer, still more cautious, decided, after re-examining the foundations, on a flat roof. Meanwhile a committee had been formed to buy up the surrounding houses and its operations have been so successful that the abbey buildings now stand in an open space visible from every side. Adjoining the south transept is the Aisle of St. Mirin built in 1499. It is roofed with a barrel vault disguised with ribs which add to its beauty, though they play no structural part. Above it a second barrel vault carries the roof. In the chapel there is a fine recumbent figure of Margery Bruce, daughter of King Robert I. The base on which it is set seems to have been made up from other tombs. Beyond St. Mirin's aisle some of the monastic buildings remain transformed into a private house by the Abercorn family in the seventeenth century. These, with the Abbey

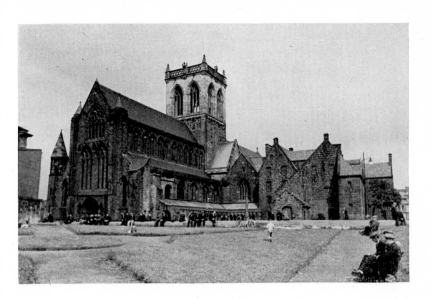

PAISLEY ABBEY

CORSTORPHINE CHURCH

PARISH CHURCH, DUNDEE

HOLY RUDE, STIRLING
Tower

47

Church, form a highly picturesque group. Other buildings lying to the west of these were unfortunately removed in 1874 to widen the street, despite a generous offer by the late Lord Bute to finance a diversion of the roadway.

The church of the preceptory of the Knights of St. John at TORPHICHEN (44) in West Lothian is a mere torso, having lost both chancel and nave. It is notable for the rooms above its vaulted transepts. With its stepped gables, angle turret and high blank walls, it looks like a cross between church and castle.

The College Church of ST. SALVATOR at ST. ANDREWS (43), built in 1450, is one of the most complete of this period. It contains the rich tomb of the founder, Bishop James Kennedy.

St. John's Church at Perth is designed with aisles for choir as well as nave ; the short transepts have no aisles. It has the low crossing characteristic of the period and this and the north porch are the only parts vaulted. The choir is a beautiful work of about 1450. The nave, built about forty years later, is of coarser work. This church, which had been subdivided and much altered, was restored by Sir Robert Lorimer.

Of the PARISH CHURCH at DUNDEE (47) only

the western tower remains. It is perhaps the finest in Scotland. Short buttresses at the corners support the vault of the lower story. Above that the walls rise unbroken in the Scots manner for the next two stories. At this point an elaborate parapet with pinnacles surrounds the tower. Within it spring two more stories crowned by another parapet and within that the gables of a rather low saddle roof. A stair turret unbroken from ground to summit completes this very striking building. It is evident from the treatment of the upper parapet that an open crown top was contemplated. It was never built and few will doubt that the present roof provides a more satisfactory finish.

The Parish CHURCH OF HOLY RUDE (48) at STIRLING is of two periods. The nave was begun about 1414. It has a fine open oak roof which was found to be in perfect condition when the plaster ceiling which had concealed it for nearly a century was removed. The lower section of the tower appears to be of the same date. The choir was built between 1507 and 1520 and the upper stages of the tower were probably added at that time. The roof of the choir aisles has been lowered and what were once triforium openings

CHURCH OF HOLY RUDE, STIRLING
The Apse

48

49   SETON COLLEGIATE CHURCH

have become windows. The five-sided apse is built against the east wall of the chancel as at Linlithgow. Both inside and out this apse is an outstanding feature and has a rugged magnificence which it would be hard to match in any other country in work of this period. The imposing effect seems to depend a good deal on the stepping down of the windows, the simple perpendicular tracery and the numerous set-offs in the buttresses. The tower has the same quality, but arrived at in a different way. The upper stories are set back as at Dundee, but only on the north and south sides. The treatment here is altogether more severe. The west side has been spoilt by the removal of the west door and lengthening of the window. This is to be put right in the present restoration when the nave and choir, used since 1656 as separate churches, are to be thrown into one. When this work is complete Holy Rude will resume its place as one of the finest parish churches in Scotland. The treatment of the crossing, which was never completed and has been much altered, presents the restorer with a difficult problem of which a satisfactory solution may necessitate some departure from the old design.

Let us now turn to the Collegiate Churches.

The more important of these were cruciform. If we compare four of the best preserved it will be found that they vary a good deal in their arrangements but all conform to an easily recognizable type, marked by conspicuous roof, low side walls and total absence of aisles. It is the same type that we saw in the three churches described at the end of the last chapter. The only difference is that the later examples lack the groined vaulting and rich mouldings of the earlier.

The COLLEGIATE CHURCH of SETON (49) in East Lothian has a chancel and eastern apse of the fifteenth century. The chancel has a barrel vault which is neatly adjusted to the apse and decorated with surface ribs. The transepts with barrel roofs and groined cornices were built by the widow of the Lord Seton who was killed at Flodden in 1513. Above the crossing is a spire still unfinished. The vaults are supported by buttresses. The nave was never built. The COLLEGIATE CHURCH of DUNGLASS (42), also in East Lothian, is similar in plan, except that there is no apse and that the buttresses are less conspicuous. There is a central tower but the crossing was not vaulted, the floors of the tower being of wood. The COLLEGIATE CHURCH of LADYKIRK (50) in

Left:
TORPHICHEN
CHURCH,
TRANSEPTS

Below:
LADYKIRK

TULLIBARDINE COLLEGIATE CHURCH

Berwickshire, built in 1500, has an unbroken barrel vault extending over nave and chancel. The short transepts have barrel vaults and separate roofs. They communicate with the nave by low arches. The transepts as well as the chancel terminate in apses and there is a western tower.

The COLLEGIATE CHURCH of TULLIBARDINE (51) in Perthshire differs from Ladykirk in having no apses and no vaults. It is a most interesting church, remaining exactly as it was built in 1446 with its roof of oak rafters placed close together, its old door and even the wooden straps on which the chancel tapestry was hung. It has a small western tower.

The COLLEGIATE CHURCH of CORSTORPHINE (46) was extended soon after it was built. It retains its old roofs and a number of fine monuments of the Forrester family.

Alongside of these cruciform churches others were being built which had neither transepts nor tower. They were usually long and narrow and the junction of nave and chancel was marked by no break in the roof, though internally they were separated by a rood screen. There was usually a belfry on the west gable. There were windows facing east, west and south, but few or

none facing north. This type was not new. At
AUCHINDOIR (11) in Aberdeenshire there is an example which dates back to the thirteenth century
and still retains a fine door of that period. Of the
period we are considering good examples will be
found at Foulis Wester near Crieff and FOULIS
EASTER (52) near Dundee. The former has recently
been carefully renovated. The latter, built about
1450, though rather cruelly restored some years
ago, is of great interest. The doors of the rood
screen have been preserved, though not in their
old position, also the sacrament house and part
of the font, and a remarkable series of paintings
on panel. The jougs still hang beside the south
door. The sacrament house or wall press where
the Host was reserved was an important feature in
late fifteenth-century churches, especially in the
north-eastern counties. It was placed in the
north-east corner of the chancel, usually in the
north wall, but occasionally as here, in the east
wall beside the altar. It was fitted with a wooden
door and surrounded with more or less elaborate
stone carvings in which the Annunciation was a
favourite subject. One of the finest examples is at
Deskford in Banffshire. The only ambry which has
retained its original door is at Stobhall near Perth.

FOULIS EASTER,
SCREEN DOORS OF 15th CENTURY

STOBHALL AMBRY,
WITH ANCIENT DOOR

52   FOULIS EASTER,
JOUGS ON WALL OF KIRK

53   Above: DRAINIE CHURCH
       Below: MICHAELKIRK

This simple and rather barn-like type of church continued to be built even after the Reformation, though slightly modified to suit the Presbyterian service. The pulpit stood in the centre of the church against the south wall. At each side of it were windows and doors symmetrically arranged. On the north side, opposite the pulpit, there was a wing which often contained a gallery. Only the orientation and the belfry on the west gable continued the pre-Reformation tradition. DRAINIE CHURCH (53) near Elgin is a typical example. It was built in 1666. The segmental arch twenty-four feet wide by which the wing opens into the church is a beautiful piece of masonry. The tracing of the windows is simple and good and so are the door mouldings. Half a mile or less from Drainie there is an even later example dated 1703. It is known as MICHAELKIRK (53). It has a large window at each end and a central door on the south flanked by two smaller windows. This singular building was intended for a burial place, so the design is not governed by the pulpit. The proportions are most pleasing, and even the urns which crown the gables do not seem out of keeping with the Gothic windows below them. In the end, though this lies outside our period, the Gothic windows disappeared altogether and were replaced by ordinary square-headed sash windows, though the plan remained substantially unaltered. At ALNESS and EDDERTON in Ross-shire and FARR, (54) in Sutherland, the eighteenth-century churches of this type are still in use. They were equipped with rooms for the minister and laird and had galleries at both ends as well as in the projection opposite the pulpit.

The COLLEGIATE CHURCH of ROSSLYN (55) stands by itself. It has none of the austerity of those we have been considering. It is but a fragment of the larger church intended, but it has a complexity of design and elaboration of ornament quite unlike any other Scots building of the mid-fifteenth century. The plan, a choir with aisles on north, south and east and chapels beyond the eastern aisle, seems to have been suggested by Glasgow Cathedral. Was the nave ever built? Of the transepts only the eastern walls exist to-day. The choir is spanned by a pointed barrel vault and this is covered with stone slabs laid directly on the vault and following its curve. The aisles are roofed by a series of barrel vaults at right angles to the axis of the building. They are supported on flat arches which span the aisles at every pier.

54

Above: ALNESS KIRK
Centre: FARR KIRK
Below: EDDERTON KIRK

ROSSLYN COLLEGIATE CHURCH
Pinnacles of South Aisle

55 ROSSLYN COLLEGIATE CHURCH
Carvings in South Aisle

These arches look at first sight like beams, being elaborately carved, but on closer scrutiny are seen to be composed of a number of stones cut in the form of voussoirs with a wraggle, a device often used in the domestic fireplaces of this period. The chapels beyond the eastern aisle have groined vaults with carved ribs and heavy pendants. This part of the church, which includes the famous 'prentice pillar, is a riot of ornament. All manner of biblical and lay subjects are represented. Much of the carving is beautiful and its richness and ingenuity impress many people. Others are rather oppressed by its profusion—the same kind of profusion which marred early Victorian decoration. The outside has the same exuberance, but the design is here held together by the long line of the roof with its curved sides and the succession of pinnacles and flying buttresses. Whatever view may be taken of its design the craftsmanship of this building must compel admiration. As a whole it is perhaps the greatest architectural curiosity in Scotland. Not the least curious detail is a full-size drawing of one of the aisle windows, incised in fine but very distinct lines on the wall of the sacristy. The church was built by Sir William Sinclair,

Earl of Orkney, between 1446 and 1484. The engrailed cross of the St. Clairs is freely used in its decoration.

The oldest woodwork remaining in Scotland belongs to this period. It is but a scanty remnant. In the larger churches almost nothing is left. At Dunblane there are a few stalls but the only building in which the woodwork is fairly complete is the CHAPEL of KING'S COLLEGE, Aberdeen (56). In ST. NICHOLAS' CHURCH (56) there are some interesting fragments but most of these belong to the seventeenth century. A great part of the woodwork and furniture used in Scotland was imported from the low countries, and the design is so much influenced by the traditions of central Europe that it is difficult to separate the native from the foreign. At Melrose the stalls were imported ready made from Bruges. Mr. J. S. Richardson, whose knowledge of these matters is unrivalled, thinks that the carved panels at King's College may have been imported and framed up here. The design certainly looks as if it might have been dependent on units which had to be worked in. The agreement for making the Glasgow stalls is preserved in the Cathedral Register, but the meaning of some of the terms is doubtful and

56   ABERDEEN

Above: KING'S COLLEGE, STALLS IN CHAPEL

Below: ST. NICHOLAS' CHURCH, SEAT OF BAXTERS'
       GUILD, 1607

CULLEN CHURCH, OGILVIE MONUMENT, 1554
AND SACRAMENT HOUSE

CULLEN CHURCHYARD

unhappily no fragment remains from which the design could be reconstructed in detail. At Kilbirnie, Pitsligo and elsewhere there are interesting family pews of the seventeenth century and in Cullen Church, Banffshire, a similar pew is constructed from panels which were originally part of the woodwork of the sittings in the body of the church.

Scattered through the churches of Scotland there are many fine monuments, some of which go back to the fifteenth century. Nearly all are slightly barbaric in character, especially those in the Highlands. Nothing like the monument of Alexander Ogilvie in CULLEN CHURCH (57) or the MacLeod monument at ROWDIL (6), with their curious survival of Gothic forms could, for instance, be found in any country but Scotland. In the matter of lettering, Scots sculptors have always been distinguished for their fine taste. Nothing could be more perfect than the fifteenth century inscriptions in Cullen Church and the same fine tradition continued to the end of the seventeenth century. We may mention in passing that the churchyard at Cullen contains a remarkable collection of table-shaped tombs.

CHAPTER VII

CASTLES OF THE FIRST PERIOD
1200–1286

Of pre-Christian defensive and domestic buildings little need be said here. With one exception they concern the antiquary more than the architect. Their remains, though numerous especially in the islands, are scanty, and their date and history can only be inferred from the tools and pottery found in them and the skeletons of their inhabitants. These suffice to prove that before the time of the earliest Christian settlement a wave of migration had swept up the west coast of Europe from the Mediterranean. This is not so surprising as at first sight appears, since by hugging the coast of Spain, France and England, the journey from Gibraltar to Shetland can be made in a small boat without losing sight of land.

The one type of prehistoric building which claims mention is the Broch, which is found nowhere except in Scotland. The best preserved examples at Mousa in Shetland, Dun Telve

in Glenelg and Dun Carloway in the Isle of
Lewis have a certain architectural importance.
They are circular towers up to fifty feet high,
tapered on the outside and built of dry stones.
They consist of a thick wall surrounding a small
court. A staircase in the thickness of the wall
curves up to the summit. This stair pierces
several passages which run horizontally round the
tower. There is no entrance to these passages
except where the stair rises through them leaving
one side open and blocking the other. They have
no windows and their walls are left very rough.
It is therefore inferred that their primary object
was to facilitate the construction of the walls and
save materials. The idea is that the builders
stood in the passage and built the walls on either
side so far as they could reach. They then
roofed the passage over with horizontal slabs
which served to bind the walls together and provided a platform for constructing the next section. The entrance to the tower was by a low
door. The central space must have been the
main dwelling though the passages may also
have been used. The walls are perpendicular
on the inner side, but set back at intervals to
afford support for floors and roof. These were

further supported by pillars which surrounded a central opening which admitted light and allowed smoke to escape. Of the origin of these strange buildings nothing is known, but the objects discovered in them indicate a date earlier than the Christian era and prove that they were in some cases occupied for several hundred years.

The Romans left many interesting traces of their occupation in Scotland, but nothing of architectural significance.

We have seen that many of the great abbeys were founded in the eleventh and twelfth centuries and that some of the finest existing buildings date from that period. It seems strange that no secular buildings of equal age, such as are found immediately over the border, should survive but this is the case. Before the Norman conquest the typical English fortress consisted of earthworks crowned by wooden palisades, the abode of the owner, also of wood, being perched on a mound or mote dominating the enclosure. The Normans, great builders in stone, soon replaced these primitive fortresses by stone castles. In Scotland the timber type seems to have persisted all through the twelfth century. Both Alexander I and David I in their efforts to extend the power of the crown, are known to have built castles in the first half of that century. Had they been of the same massive masonry as the churches, it is inconceivable that no trace should be left.

The thirteenth century saw one of the few calm interludes in Scotland's troubled history. The reigns of Alexander II and his son extended from 1214 to 1286 and during these seventy-two years the country enjoyed greater prosperity than at any other period before the Union. Both the Alexanders made English marriages and peace between the two countries permitted them to devote their energies to the consolidation of their own kingdom. Within its narrow boundaries four more or less hostile races had to be reconciled, the Scots in Argyll, the Picts in the north and east, the Welsh in Strathclyde and the Saxons in the Lothians and border counties. Moreover the Norse invaders, who still occupied the western isles and several settlements on the mainland, had to be expelled. This formidable undertaking, begun by Malcolm Canmore nearly two hundred years earlier, had been greatly simplified by the introduction of the feudal system under his son David I and the bestowal of large tracts of land on Saxon and Norman immigrants from whom many of the great historical families in Scotland are descended.

Alexander II subdued Argyll and the Highlands as far as Caithness and repelled a Norse invasion in 1230. He died during an attempt to recover the Hebrides. His son offered to buy the Hebrides from King Haakon who responded by sending a powerful fleet to the Clyde which attempted a landing at Largs in 1263. Here the Norsemen were defeated and their ships wrecked in a storm. Thus ended an occupation which had lasted four and a half centuries. The Hebrides were regained and three years later the Isle of Man was also added to Scotland.

The feudal system, which had made these acquisitions possible, also assisted their consolidation. Grants of land were made to earls and barons (an earldom included several baronies) in return for which a certain number of armed men had to be available for the service of the crown. The tenants who paid their rents partly in kind and partly in service were called on for this duty. The earliest stone castles in Scotland belong to this period. The fortress was an integral part of the feudal system. It was not only a place of safety, but a symbol of the owner's dignity and importance and his ordinary residence. By this time stone castles had been in use for more than a century in France and England and the Saxon and Norman barons who settled in Scotland must have been familiar with them.

The early Scots castles are very simple in plan, consisting in many cases of a plain four-sided enclosure surrounded by walls twenty to forty feet high and eight to ten feet thick. They had no windows. The enclosures vary greatly in size, but were seldom less than eighty to a hundred yards square. In shape they conformed to the site which consisted usually of a low rocky table, promontory or island, or a piece of dry ground surrounded by swamps. At the angles, towers, usually round, were often placed. These contained several floors reached by stairs which also led to the battlements which crowned the walls. Any other accommodation must have been in lean-to buildings surrounding the enclosure. The entrance was by a fairly wide arch defended by a portcullis.

INVERLOCHY CASTLE (58) is a good example of this type. It has circular towers at each corner. One, called Comyn's Tower, is larger than the others. The rooms in it were twenty feet across and the walls are over ten feet thick. The stair, as in the other towers, is in the thickness of the wall and follows its curve. There were two entrances to this castle on opposite sides. Comyn's Tower is a modest version of the great tower at Coucy in France.

DUNSTAFFNAGE CASTLE (58) is more imposing and more attractive on account of its enchanting site, irregular shape and sixteenth-century additions. Here the plan, four-sided though by no means square, conforms strictly to the outline of the rock on which it stands. The circular angle towers have scarcely any projection. The walls rise sheer from their rocky base with majestic effect. The hereditary Captain still holds this castle from the Duke of Argyll. Nearby are the ruins of a beautiful thirteenth-century chapel which formed an appanage of the stronghold.

Both these castles, like many others in the Highlands, are crude versions of the type of fortress found at this period in France and England but they have a distinctly Scots flavour. Others in masonry, design and scale approach much closer to their foreign models. Of these Bothwell, Dirleton and Kildrummy are outstanding examples.

58   Above: INVERLOCHY CASTLE
Below: DUNSTAFFNAGE CASTLE

59 Above: SPYNIE PALACE, GATEWAY
  Below: DUNSTAFFNAGE, THIRTEENTH CENTURY CHAPEL

BOTHWELL CASTLE (60) belonged in the thirteenth century to the family of De Moravia or Murray. The great tower or donjon may, in this case, be directly related to its prototype at Coucy, since the mother of Alexander III, in whose reign it was built, was the sister of the builder of Coucy. In this type of fortress each tower was capable of being defended separately, though all communicated with the ramparts which crowned the curtain walls. The donjon at Bothwell is separated by a moat from the courtyard and its door is defended by a drawbridge and portcullis. The drawbridge was of the old type pulled up by chains. One of later type, fitted with a counterpoise, may be seen at the opposite end of the courtyard behind the fifteenth-century hall. The walls of the donjon are fifteen feet thick. The octagonal hall which occupies the ground floor is thirty-seven feet in diameter and vaulted with stone. It is, or rather was, for only half remains, the most splendid room of its kind in Scotland. Below was a cellar reached only from the hall. Above, on a level with the ramparts, was a large room lit only by loopholes, probably a store for munitions, and above that a well lighted room used by the lord of the castle. Above this again the newel stair continued to the roof, which was flat. The upper part of the tower is gone, but it was no doubt, like the Coucy tower, surrounded by corbels * carrying a wooden gallery from which the defence was conducted. This arrangement was superseded in the fourteenth century by stone battlements of which a fine example may be seen on the south-east tower which was rebuilt about 1400. Here the parapet was carried on small arches uniting the corbels, holes being left next the wall for purposes of defence.

The castle suffered severely in the Wars of Independence. It was captured by Edward I and dismantled by the Scots after its recapture in 1335. It afterwards passed into the hands of the great family of Douglas, to whose descendant, Lord Home, it still belongs. The new owners restored the north and east walls and built a new hall and chapel in the courtyard, thus bringing the accommodation up to the standard which we shall see later obtained in the early fifteenth century. This was probably the work of Archibald the Grim. The main entrance must have been in the north wall where there is now a wide gap. It

* Stone brackets.

60

BOTHWELL CASTLE
Above: Donjon
Below: South-East Tower

LOCH-AN-EILAN CASTLE

has completely disappeared. Two buttresses on the outside of this wall which supported circular turrets deserve study on account of their fine corbelling. They are early examples of a device which persisted in Scotland for 300 years, and more than any other feature distinguishes its buildings from those of other countries. The thirteenth century latrines in the south curtain wall also deserve notice. At this early period sanitation received more attention than it did in the period which followed. Here ingenious contrivances will be seen for flushing the outflow and preventing the outlet being used as an entrance.

Lord Home has recently made over the custody of this castle to H.M. Office of Works and interesting discoveries may be expected. The site, surrounded on three sides by the deep valley of the Clyde, is one of romantic beauty. Fine woods shut out the industrial surroundings. The modern house has been demolished. All round there is a large and growing population. There seems here to be an opportunity of making some day a really beautiful public park just where it is wanted. Meanwhile through the owner's kindness it plays a useful part as a quiet place of recreation of which trips and picnic parties make good use.

Bothwell has been described at some length because it is the finest castle of the period among the thirty or more which still exist in Scotland. In all of them the root idea of a large enclosure surrounded by very thick walls is apparent. Some, like Castle Roy, near Nethy Bridge, Inverness-shire, or Kinclaven, near the junction of the Isla with the Tay, Perthshire, are simple square enclosures. Others, like Inverlochy or Dunstaffnage, as we have seen, are larger and slightly more elaborate. At Rothesay, in Bute, the shape is circular. At Caerlaverock it is triangular. At Kildrummy it is an irregular but symmetrical pentagon. At Lochindorb a fairly large island was fortified. At Lochmaben a large island was created by severing a neck of land. At Loch Doon and LOCH AN EILAN (61) small islands were completely encircled. At Eilean Donan and Dunvegan, both much altered, the site was close to the sea. At Yester the enclosure was safeguarded by underground passages designed to frustrate attempts to undermine the walls. At Duffus (near Elgin) the donjon was built on the mound or mote of a more ancient castle, as often happened in England but

CAERLAVEROCK CASTLE

63   KILDRUMMY CASTLE

Above: Chapel and North-East Tower

Below: North Side, with Base of Snow Tower on Right

rarely in Scotland. These are all variants of the same idea—an enclosure as safe as labour and ingenuity could make it. At Bothwell and Kildrummy we see this idea carried out with a splendour comparable to that of the great castles of England and France.

We will conclude this chapter with a note on three of the above mentioned fortresses which have special claims to the reader's attention. KILDRUMMY CASTLE (63) is surpassed only by Bothwell among Scots thirteenth-century castles. Like Bothwell it was built by a member of the Murray family, Gilbert de Moravia, Bishop of Caithness, who was an accomplished architect and probably designed it himself. The building must have been a tremendous undertaking as it is a granite country and the material, a beautiful freestone, must have been brought from a great distance. The longest of its five sides faces north and is flanked by two round towers of which the larger, called the Snow Tower, is nearly as large as the Bothwell donjon. Dr. Mackay Mackenzie deduces from Barbour's rhymed chronicle that the Snow Tower was built or rebuilt in the fourteenth century. The other seems to have been rebuilt by the English after the castle, in consequence of a fire, capitulated to Edward I. The windows are of a type common in England, but not found elsewhere in Scotland. The east window of the chapel is a fine piece of First Pointed work. The gable which it adorns projects at an angle from the curtain wall with the object no doubt of correcting the orientation. The late owner has been criticized for rebuilding part of the Snow Tower which had been destroyed. His object was to restore the grand curve of the donjon as seen from below. In this he succeeded and criticism seems pedantic since the facts are on record and particular care was taken to distinguish the new masonry from the old. The writer wishes that the keep at Bothwell could receive the same treatment. The old masonry is of fine quality in both castles.

The triangular castle of CAERLAVEROCK (62) stands on a level site surrounded by a moat and protected by swamps. The entrance between twin towers which formed the Keep is at the north angle. The other angles are defended by smaller circular towers. The student who cares to unravel the changes a building has undergone will find this castle of great interest. At first sight it appears from outside a complete thirteenth-century castle and answers exactly to the description of Walter of Exeter, an eye-witness who took part in the siege by Edward I. On closer inspection all the towers are seen to be of fifteenth-century work. It is not even certain that they are built on the same site. Shot holes are an integral part of their design which in Scotland implies a date not earlier than 1450. The original towers were probably destroyed by the English after the capitulation of the sixty men who formed the garrison. The original doorway was deeply recessed between the flanking towers and the slit for its portcullis may still be seen behind the gate and portcullis of the fifteenth century. Any buildings which existed in the triangular courtyard at the time of the siege have been replaced by later work, mostly of the seventeenth century, very good of its kind and interesting for its heraldic and other devices. The doorway of the great hall, which faces the visitor as he enters the courtyard, is a fine example of Scots renaissance design. The ability of the architect employed on this work is shown in his frank acceptance of the awkward angles resulting from the triangular plan. It is this difficulty which has prevented the triangular plan coming into general use. When one of the angles faces north as it does at Caerlaverock there is much to be said for it, since only one wall out of six fails to get the sun at some time of the day.

LOCH DOON CASTLE (64) occupied the whole of a small island in the lonely loch of that name in the hills which separate Ayrshire from the Stewartry. It formed an enclosure with twelve unequal sides. The external masonry of the curtain wall, in strong contrast to its moorland site, is of ashlar work, every stone being beautifully wrought. The entrance was by a pointed gateway of Early English design with a portcullis and inner gate secured by sliding bars. The portcullis is in the loch, but the precise spot is not known. An attempt was made many years ago to raise it on the ice, but the ice broke and the loch again engulfed it. The position of the hall is indicated by a large ambry or recessed sideboard and a fine fireplace, both built into the wall of enceinte. The latter still retains part of its floor with the stone fender. Except for these relics, all evidence of the thirteenth-century arrangements has been obliterated by fifteenth-century additions, which included a lofty tower. This castle, like most of its period, suffered severely in the War of Independence. It was surrendered to the

English in 1306 by Sir Gilbert de Carrick in the mistaken belief that the cause of Bruce had been finally lost in the battle of Methven.

Of all Scots castles this was perhaps the most romantic in its site and surroundings and, but for man's interference with the level of the loch, would still be so. Its walls rose directly from the water until some years ago the level was lowered and more of the island exposed. Now the loch has been utilized as a reservoir for the Galloway Hydro-Electric Power Scheme. The castle was threatened with submersion, and the company to their credit have borne the expense of removing it to a site which will be above the new level. This work has been carried out at a cost of over £3,000 by the trained staff of H.M. Office of Works, who have performed their task so skilfully that a comparison stone by stone of the masonry as recorded in photographs before and after removal reveals, as the reader will see, no difference. The castle has lost charm by its removal and in a measure authenticity, but it still deserves a visit if it be only to see the perfection with which the ashlar work has been reset as a lasting record.

CHAPTER VIII

CASTLES—SECOND PERIOD
1286–1424

This will be a short chapter, the material with which it deals being comparatively scanty. With the death of Alexander III in 1286 the building of great castles, such as those described in the last chapter, came to an abrupt end. The king's death was followed by that of his granddaughter, the Maid of Norway, his only direct heir, and with the attempt of Edward I of England to set Balliol on the throne, Scotland entered on a period of war, disturbance and poverty from which she had little respite till James I returned in 1424 from his long captivity at Windsor and married an English wife. These 138 years which constitute the second period of castle building were rich in adventure and noble deeds which cluster round the names of Wallace and Bruce. They secured Scotland's independence. In everything else they were lean years. They show how completely, then as now, a nation's

LOCH DOON CASTLE
Above: BEFORE REMOVAL
Below: AFTER REMOVAL

The oblong shown within dotted lines in the upper
view corresponds with the illustration below.

65   Above: THREAVE CASTLE
Below: CARRICK CASTLE

prosperity was at the mercy of its rulers and how, then as now, the risk of misgovernment was increased and excused, if not justified, by the rivalry of its neighbours. Under Malcolm Canmore and his successors Scotland had secured a fair share of European civilization. Her buildings were comparable with those of France and England. During the Wars of Independence much of this ground was lost. Castles on the thirteenth-century model were beyond the means even of the most powerful nobles. At THREAVE (65) the Black Douglas was content with a strong square tower. The royal castle of Dundonald also consisted of a single tower. It is a pity that so little is left of these larger towers and that the Erskine stronghold at Alloa, though still standing, has been so drastically remodelled. But enough remains to show that the more important towers were very well built. It is in scale and purpose rather than technique that the troubles of the time are reflected. The need of defence against sudden raids persisted in Scotland well into the seventeenth century, and fortified dwellings continued to be built for nearly four hundred years with little change in design or construction. It is not easy to estimate the age of these towers unless the date is recorded on the building itself or elsewhere. The problem is, as usual, complicated by the fact that many of the earlier towers have either been altered or have fallen to ruin.

The origin of this type of tower has been traced to the Norman Keeps in the north of England. The reader may object that so simple a structure scarcely requires a model, being simply the resultant of the builder's needs and resources—the need of protection from attack and from fire, limited by scarcity of labour, money and skill. Experienced students will not take this view. In building, even where the purpose and materials are identical, there is so much room for variation in design that the simplest problem is hardly ever spontaneously solved twice in the same manner. The Norman type of tower was not a new importation. It was already familiar to Scots builders in the thirteenth century castles. It was now put to a rather different purpose—that of providing a fortified dwelling on a smaller scale.

These towers at their simplest were quadrangular in shape with a vaulted basement. The entrance was usually on the first floor approached by an outside stair of stone or wood. Above the vaulted basement there were one or sometimes two more vaults in the height of the tower, the spaces between which were divided by wooden floors making, with the basement, three to five stories, of which that with the door served as the hall. The wooden floors were supported on stone corbels built into the walls. The internal stairs are sometimes spiral and sometimes straight. In either case they were contained in the thickness of the wall without any projection on the outside. The walls were seven to nine feet thick in the earlier examples. The stair after giving access to the various floors led up to a turret or cape house from which one stepped out on to the roof which was protected by a crenellated parapet. At the vulnerable corners projecting rounds were corbelled out. These are often called bartizans, but that term properly belongs to the wooden projections described in the last chapter. The parapet, to give width to the roof and perhaps to aid the defence, is often slightly corbelled out, but this feature becomes more marked at a later date. The roofs of the fourteenth-century towers seem to have been nearly flat. They rested on the upper vault and were paved with overlapping flagstones. These were laid after the manner of the old fashioned half-round tiles, the lower courses being made slightly concave to carry off the rain water, while the upper, which covered the joints, were slightly convex. Great skill was put into the construction of this type of roof which was used for all kinds of buildings. Given a good stone and a vaulted support it is as nearly everlasting as anything constructed by man can be. The entrance to the tower was defended by a door and inside it by an iron yett. Before the end of this period the accommodation in the towers was increased by raising the roof to a steeper pitch with gables at either end. These rested on the inner face of the walls so as to leave room for a flagged walk on every side behind the parapet.

These towers provided more accommodation than one would at first sight suppose. The hall occupied the whole of the entrance floor, but the upper floors were subdivided by partitions. This would give seven rooms at least besides the basement. There were, no doubt, also outbuildings in the small courts or enclosures which were invariably attached to the tower though often only the foundations of their enclosing walls now remain. In the smaller towers, such as that of Loch Leven (66) the kitchen was probably in an

66   Above: LOCH LEVEN CASTLE
Below: HERMITAGE CASTLE

PRESTON TOWER

COXTON TOWER

outside building. At Threave it occupied an entresol below the hall. At Crichton in Midlothian, where a fourteenth-century tower is embedded in a later castle, a small kitchen was contrived in the same position in the haunch of the vault. A few of the larger towers of this period such as Neidpath on the Tweed or the tower which forms the nucleus of Craigmillar had projecting wings making them L-shaped. This added greatly to the number of rooms and convenience of access, especially where the wing was contrived with more stories than the main building. In every case there were a number of small apartments in the thickness of the wall. The dry closets or garde robes, as they are usually termed, were always in this position. Sometimes they were provided with internal flues, but more often were projected on corbels which enabled the effluents to fall more or less clear of the wall.

It is difficult for us to visualize life in these towers. It cannot have been luxurious. It must have been wanting in privacy. But it was probably a good deal more comfortable than would appear to those who see them in ruins. None of the early towers remain in their original state, but some of the later, such as Coxton, are still intact and provide a vivid picture of life in a small tower. From them it would appear that the external walls when built with rubble were usually covered with harling and thus rendered weatherproof. There is no evidence that harling was used before the fifteenth century, and the earlier towers are usually built with dressed stones. The inside walls were certainly plastered and in the upper stories the partitions, which have now disappeared, were of wood or lath and plaster. The floors were covered with rushes, bent grass and birch twigs. The stone seats in the window recesses—a charming and constant feature—were no doubt fitted with cushions. The windows themselves were filled with glass in the upper half while the lower opened with shutters. This treatment persisted well into the seventeenth century. It is found at Saughton Mills in 1623 and in the Place of Paisley even later. A good specimen was discovered not long ago at the Inch, Midlothian, when a built-up window was reopened. Life in these towers must have been rather like life on board ship or in a sleeping car. After all there is a good deal to be said for a cabin ten feet by eight in which everything is within easy reach. People were as intelligent then as they are now and though our elaborate standard fittings were not available, our forebears no doubt had very efficient dodges of their own for making the most of the small space at their disposal.

CHAPTER IX

CASTLES—THIRD PERIOD
1424–1550

For a century after 1424 Scotland was free from foreign aggression and though the country was still disturbed by domestic quarrels there was more building with more variety in design. Castle building in Scotland was so conservative, the same forms persisted for so long, that the reader must not hope for a sharp distinction between this period and the next. He may find the word medieval helpful. Life in Scotland during this period was distinctly medieval, though towards its close modern ideas began to appear. In the next it was definitely modern, though in the earlier years traces of medievalism survived. The domestic changes which accompanied this transition are reflected in the buildings and their furniture, and failing documentary evidence form the best criterion of their date.

All through this period castles of tower form were still being built. Those of the smaller lairds followed closely the models we have been considering and are scarcely distinguishable from them except by their thinner walls, improved accommodation and the evolution of certain features. The corbelling, for instance, which carried the parapet in the earlier examples consisted of a continuous moulding or a single row of corbels. Later, for the sake of ornament, a second row was often added. If the corbels were separate they alternated with those in the row above it and became, with their crisp shadows, an effective element in the design. Shot holes began to appear about the middle of the fifteenth century, and, for a period, embrasures for cannon, though these were soon discarded as impractical. The earlier shot holes were widely splayed on the outside, but the splay attracted the enemy's attention and bullets, and was replaced in later buildings by the smallest possible aperture, the splay being confined to the inside.

Elphinstone Castle in Midlothian is a well preserved example of a plain four-sided fifteenth-century tower. Its walls are honeycombed with small rooms which must have added greatly to the comfort and privacy of its inhabitants. The entrance is on the ground floor with the usual guardroom and prison in the thickness of the wall. A straight stair, also built in the thickness of the wall, leads to the hall, at the end of which is a small kitchen. The mural chambers, which complicate the plan too much for description here —there are no less than fifteen of them—were entered from the window recesses and from three newel stairs which led from the hall to the upper floors. One of these chambers, the private room of the owner or his wife, has a window overlooking the hall. This is contrived by means of a double opening across the flue of the hall chimney. The design of this tower is admittedly exceptional. In attempting to supply within the four walls of a square tower the accommodation now looked for in the larger castles, it carried the expedient of the mural chamber beyond its legitimate limit and must have rendered the building almost useless as a fortress. It is described here because it illustrates the growing demand for more space and greater privacy.

Affleck Castle in Angus is a smaller, simpler, and rather later example. It has a square projection at one corner which contains the principal stair. The L-shaped plan, of which we saw an example at Craigmillar, built before 1400, soon became so popular that it may be fairly described as the normal form of the moderately sized Scots castle or house for nearly three hundred years. Like the Elphinstone tower, this tower at Affleck has two stories below the hall, of which the upper is vaulted, but the hall itself, as well as the two upper stories, has a wooden ceiling. Above the principal stair, which does not ascend beyond the hall, there is a small private room forming an entresol and above it a chapel opening from the room above the hall. Here, as at Elphinstone, there is a peep into the hall, but in this case it is contrived from a garderobe adjoining the private room. The battlements have square machicolated projections on each face and projecting rounds at each corner except that occupied by the cape-house of the secondary staircase which gives access to the battlements. The parapets have unfortunately been restored without embrasures. The Castle of Mains in Lanarkshire may be cited as an example of a plain tower dating from the end of this period. Here again the shell is complete, except for the battlements.

Larger towers of the period are Comlongan Castle in Dumfriesshire, which contains some fine Gothic details, and EDZELL (119) in Angus. CARRICK CASTLE (65) on the lonely shore of Loch Goil is remarkable for its fine masonry and for the fact that all its ceilings were of wood. Its date is unknown and it is doubtful whether it should be placed in this or the preceding period. Argyllshire has several other towers of this date, of which Dunolly, near Oban, and the seagirt Castle Stalcaire are familiar to every tourist.

Alongside with these modest buildings, fortresses on a larger scale were being built. Some, like BORTHWICK CASTLE (68) with its great twin square projections, HERMITAGE (66) with still more salient wings and Crookston with four square towers attached to a central block may be reckoned as developments of the tower idea. Borthwick and Hermitage are perhaps the most imposing buildings in Scotland. They, as well as Crookston, were built of dressed stone and never harled. Their halls were noble rooms with vaulted roofs, stately fireplaces and tall deep windows fitted with stone seats. They were provided with ambries or cupboards recessed into the wall and sometimes, as at Borthwick and Sauchie in Clackmannanshire, with stone wash basins. At HUNTINGTOWER (70), the old Perth-

BORTHWICK CASTLE
Above: From a photograph by R. M. Adam
Below: From a drawing by R. W. Billings

69   GREAT HALL, BORTHWICK CASTLE

shire home of the Ruthvens, there are twin towers standing close together. When one tower proved too small it was found more convenient to build another than to add to the first. The same contrivance was used at the Dean in Ayrshire and at Mochrum in Galloway.

So much for the tower and its development, of which we shall see the final phase in the next chapter. We have now to consider a quite different type of castle which first emerges in this period— the castle whose buildings were grouped round a courtyard. This change of plan was made in response to the demand for more and larger rooms. The hall was retained with increased splendour as the principal apartment. It was often a separate building with large windows, a dais and screen and an open roof like the English halls of the same date. It was sufficiently important to give its name to a new class of building —the palace—in Latin 'palatium' which means no more than hall.

In addition to the hall, private dining and sitting rooms now began to be required, answering to the public rooms of a modern country house, and bedrooms in increased numbers. It is impossible to estimate exactly the accommodation provided in the great castles of this date, of which Doune, Tantallon, Dunnottar, Craigmillar, Crichton, Castle Campbell and Craignethan are fine examples, not to mention Spynie, the fortified palace of the Bishops of Moray. All these were built at more than one date and are full of compromises between old and new ideas. It also happens that the subsidiary buildings in the courtyard have in every case been destroyed or altered beyond recognition. These castles were designed with elaborate defences and were certainly intended to resist any sudden attack. How far their towers, gateways and battlements were relied on for protection in war and how far they were mere emblems of the owner's rank and power we cannot tell, but comparing them with the earlier fortresses one feels that from a military point of view they cannot, after the invention of gunpowder, have been taken very seriously.

DOUNE CASTLE (75) in Perthshire, built by the Regent Albany in the first quarter of the fifteenth century, is as nearly even aged as any, but even here there are compromises and awkward adjustments which suggest that the design is not a considered whole. After the Regent's execution in 1424 this castle lapsed to the Crown and was given by James IV to Queen Margaret through whom it returned to the Stewart family. Its interest is greatly increased by the fact that it still belongs to the Earl of Moray. On the main floor the castle has two large public rooms reached from the courtyard by outside stairs, a vaulted hall over the gateway and adjoining it a larger banqueting hall with an open timber roof. Beyond the larger hall is a kitchen set at an angle to the other buildings. The triangular space between them was used as a service room (75) and is provided with a wide counter for dishes with two large openings to the kitchen. The main entrance to the banqueting hall was through this room. The door gave into the space behind the screens over which there was a gallery for musicians. A stair from the cellar also entered the hall behind the screens. This rather crude version of the arrangements usual in English halls was necessitated by the limits of the site. There is no fireplace in the banqueting hall. There may have been a fire in the centre of the floor though such an inconvenient arrangement seems unlikely at this date. The other hall and the drawing room and private room above it are all provided with good fireplaces. It was probably in this gateway block that the owner and his family lived. It contains a small chapel. The kitchen block is also carried up to form a tower which provided accommodation for guests. The remaining sides of the courtyard are enclosed with high walls. Any buildings which abutted against them have been destroyed if they were ever built. Judging from the window openings important additions, perhaps including a larger chapel, seem to have been contemplated. Seen from any angle this castle is a noble pile. There is a pleasant proportion in the design which can scarcely have been accidental. On the other hand there is no trace of any desire for symmetry, in the modern sense of correspondence of parts, such as is found in buildings of the same or earlier date in England. The whole building is definitely Scots.

TANTALLON (70), the great stronghold of the Red Douglas, is about fifty years older than Doune and strictly speaking belongs to the last period. It is placed here as the immediate precursor of the fifteenth-century courtyard castles, though it actually follows rather the plan of the thirteenth. Three sides were defended by the sea. On the fourth a great curtain wall was built across the isthmus strengthened by towers at each end and

CRAIGMILLAR CASTLE

TANTALLON CASTLE

HUNTINGTOWER

CASTLE CAMPBELL

another in the centre over the gateway. The hall and kitchen were in a range of buildings at right angles to this great screen. Craignethan Castle, Scott's Tillietudlem, which stands among deep woods on a steep spur in a lovely side valley of the Clyde, is built on quite a different plan. The main building here is a massive tower containing the hall and a number of other rooms. Around it a courtyard has been constructed at a slightly later date rather cramped by the narrow site but defended by very strong walls on which guns have been mounted, and towers, one of which is large enough to have provided a good deal of accommodation. A wide ditch cut across the salient on which the castle stands completed its defence. The outer courtyard beyond this ditch seems to have been an afterthought. It contains some delightful buildings of the sixteenth and seventeenth centuries. At CRAIGMILLAR (70), Crichton and CASTLE CAMPBELL (71), fourteenth century towers form the cores of later courtyard castles, but the additions were made at so many different times that they illustrate, not one period, but many. For that reason they are not described at length here, but for the same reason abundantly repay a visit. Individually they have features of great interest such as the loggia at Castle Campbell, the renaissance staircase at Crichton, and at Craigmillar the fine range of private rooms linked up with the old hall in the tower.

At SPYNIE (59), the largest and best built fortress of this period, a tower of six stories survives, with hall, prison, etc. Also remnants of lesser towers and a chapel. A singularly fine gate-way, bearing until recently the arms of John Innes, consecrated bishop in 1406, may be of the second period.

The accommodation in these castles shows a great advance on that in the towers described in the last chapter, but many things which we consider essential to comfort were still wanting. In the hall of an ordinary private house there was only one chair with back and arms—that of the head of the house. Everyone else had to be content with stools and benches. There were no couches or sofas, and no small tables. From the earliest times, beds are important items in the inventories but the bedding was more important than the frame. Mr. Warrack tells us that the first mention of a four poster occurs in 1539 though before that date there were canopies with curtains suspended from the ceiling. The box bed did not come into use till the end of the sixteenth century.

For the full expression of the architectural ideals of the period we must turn to the royal palaces. The Castles of Edinburgh and Stirling both contain palaces of this date. The palaces of Linlithgow and Falkland were both built as such.

EDINBURGH CASTLE (12) has been a royal residence since the time of Malcolm Canmore. David II added a large tower of which the lower part may still be seen behind the half-moon battery. At the corner of the rock behind this the Stewart kings added a block of buildings, now much altered, of which the fine hall with its timber roof alone remains fairly intact. The destruction of the castle dates from the siege of 1572 when it was held for Queen Mary by Kirkcaldy of Grange against the Regent Morton. The castle in its present form is mainly the work of the same Regent after the capitulation. STIRLING CASTLE (72) has far more of interest both for architect and historian. The older buildings have been destroyed, burnt or altered, but the palace group added in the fifteenth century is fairly complete. The parliament hall, which is isolated from the other buildings, seems to be the work of James III. With its beautiful oriels, deeply recessed segmental windows and fine dimensions, 125 feet by 36, this must have been a very noble room. It is maddening to think that its open timber roof was still intact at the beginning of the nineteenth century, when it was converted into barracks. The double towered inner gateway is of the same date as the hall. The palace block which almost adjoins the hall is built round a small central court. Here James IV, the builder, is said to have kept lions. It is still known as the lion's den. The entrance to the principal floor is at the north-west corner. It leads on the left to two large reception rooms of which the second was the presence chamber. This room had a ceiling carved in oak which was taken down in 1771 when the carvings were dispersed. They comprised a series of circular panels with heads carved in relief after the manner of the early Italian renaissance. The designs are recorded not very accurately in a volume entitled *Lacunar Strivelense*, Edinburgh, Blackwood, 1817. A good many of these carvings survive in private houses and public collections. As this was one of the most important examples of woodwork in Scotland it seems highly desirable that the remnants should be brought together and the ceiling reconstructed in

STIRLING CASTLE, PALACE AND INNER GATE

STIRLING CASTLE, PALACE FROM OUTER COURT

FALKLAND PALACE
Right: Courtyard
Below: Gateway

its original position. The other rooms on this floor comprise a drawing room and dining room and two smaller private rooms all leading one from another without any passage or doors to the court. The tower attached to the south side of the block is of earlier date and is probably the oldest building in the castle. The rooms have been subdivided for military purposes. If they were cleared out much of interest might come to light. The exterior of the palace is the most complete example of early renaissance work which survives in Scotland. It may be crude judged by Italian or French or even English standards. The scholar may resent the prominence given to ornaments designed originally for subsidiary positions. But in its originality, its agreeable proportion and even in its faults, the building is intensely Scots and illustrates in a delightful way the first hesitant approach of the renaissance to a distant country still steeped in the Gothic tradition. Sir Robert Lorimer's quick eye borrowed from its design, not too happily perhaps, for the main block of the National Memorial in Edinburgh Castle. With the late Gothic hall it forms the most interesting group of its period in Scotland. Its present condition is a disgrace to us.

The Jacobean Chapel, built by James VI for the christening of Henry, Prince of Wales, in 1594, which forms the north side of the same courtyard is about to be put in order with the sanction of H.M. Office of Works for the Church of Scotland. The writer knows that the department is eager to tackle its more important neighbours. It is a formidable undertaking since it involves the provision of new buildings for military purposes, but it is one which is long overdue and which public opinion would certainly support.

It is interesting to compare the PALACE OF FALKLAND (73) with that of Stirling. The side facing the street is Gothic in design and no doubt a little earlier than the renaissance work at Stirling. The buttresses, an unusual feature in Scotland, may have been deemed necessary to reinforce the narrow sections of wall between the large windows. The entrance between two circular towers closely resembles the gate at Stirling and the north-west wing of Holyroodhouse, but has no portcullis. At Stirling the palace was within a fortress and there was no occasion for defence. Here, though the old defensive forms are retained, including shot holes flanking the entrance, the building is evidently not seriously intended for defence. The side facing the courtyard consists of a gallery added by James V to the older building. It bears his arms and those of Mary of Guise and must have been built between 1539 when they were married and 1542 when the king died. Its elevation shows the renaissance design carried a step further than at Stirling. It has the same faults and the same merits. The work at Falkland is more scholarly than that at Stirling, but less bold and less distinctively Scots. French masons are known to have been in the employment of James IV and James V. If this is their work, they probably drew their designs from books or from details sketched from other buildings.

The main block contains the hall and three smaller rooms on the principal floor. The hall has retained its old screen (77) wrought with balusters in finely grained Scots oak. The rest of the palace has disappeared and the large additions made by James VI are in ruins. It was in an earlier building that the Duke of Rothesay was starved to death in 1402 by the Regent Albany to whom Falkland then belonged.

We have left to the last the most imposing residence of the Scots kings, the PALACE OF

LINLITHGOW (74). It is on a larger scale than those we have described and in that respect perhaps less characteristic of Scotland. It is also more of a fortress. Certain details such as the Tudor windows in the courtyard, with their groups of arched and cusped lights framed in an elaborate moulding, are frankly borrowed from England. So are the mullions and transoms on the Jacobean north front. But the pile as seen from outside, though simpler in mass than most Scots buildings, is made up of features which unmistakably proclaim its nationality. The corner towers, with their corbelled battlements and projecting rounds and crow-stepped gables, could belong to no other country, nor could the deeply recessed windows of the hall and chapel.

The old castle which occupied this site, like those of Edinburgh and Stirling, seems to have been rendered untenable by Robert the Bruce during his struggle with the English. It was repaired by David II, but burnt in 1424. The earliest of the existing buildings date from the reign of James I who began the narrow range on the west side which was completed in 1451. The oriel window near the north-west corner is of this date. The chapel and great hall which occupy most of the

LINLITHGOW PALACE
Above: View from South-West
Below: Great Hall

DOUNE CASTLE

DOUNE CASTLE, SERVICE ROOM

south and east ranges must have been built in the second half of the fifteenth century. They are good examples of late Gothic work without a trace of the renaissance ornaments which came into vogue about 1500. The corner staircases and passages of the south range facing the court seem to have been the work of James V in the early sixteenth century. The south entrance by which visitors usually enter is also his work. The older and finer entrance is on the east and passes under the great hall. Its decorations both outside and in are notable examples of the lovely last phase of Gothic. Scotland must have had some admirable artists at that time. One wonders whether the same men were responsible for the renaissance designs at Stirling and Falkland. It is difficult to believe that they were. One wonders also what part may have been played by Sir James Hamilton, the Bastard of Arran, who had spent his early years at the court of Francis I and was James V's official architect and intimate friend till his disgrace and execution in 1540. He is said to have superintended that king's work at Linlithgow and Falkland, as well as the building of his brother's castle of Craignethan.* The

* *Dictionary of National Biography.*

north side of the court was rebuilt by King James VI. It is a good example of its kind and cleverly united to the older work. It will remind the reader of similar work at Caerlaverock.

Mary of Guise, who knew the great houses of France, is credited with saying of Linlithgow that she had never seen a more princely palace. She did not expect the wide staircases or succession of great rooms which made the palaces of the next generation convenient as well as splendid. She may never have seen the palace of the Popes at Avignon with its immense white halls or the castle at Naples. But she knew the Tuilleries and Fontainebleau and the work of Le Muet and the Du Cerceaux. Judged by the standards of her day, when the parts of a palace were more important than the whole, Linlithgow is not wanting. The great hall with its triple fireplace (74), its long perspective of tall windows and brackets for statues, the chapel, the long dining room and airy drawing room must all have been noble pieces. The new staircases and corridors added for the Queen's comfort had made it possible to get to any part of the building without going out of doors. The doors and entries may have been low and narrow, but they preserved the human scale too often lost in the pompous buildings of a later date and by contrast must have enhanced the sense of space and freedom in the lofty rooms. How one wishes that this old home of the kings of Scotland had come down to us intact, with its woodwork and windows, and the tapestries and furniture which accompanied the king on his visits. A restoration is said to have been contemplated when Queen Victoria required a residence in Scotland. If we may judge by Balmoral, Linlithgow had a lucky escape. But a restoration now would be a very different thing and to the writer it seems worth contemplating, not as a royal habitation, but as a home for the furniture, tapestries and portraits which look so unhappy in museums. The building is steeped in history. All the Stewart kings lived here. The luckless Queen Mary was born here. The body of Regent Moray, shot by Hamilton of Bothwellhaugh, was brought here after his death at the inn in the town.

HOLYROODHOUSE (76) and Dunfermline complete the list of royal palaces. At Holyrood the old monastic buildings have entirely disappeared, as well as the additions made to them by James IV. The earliest existing building, except of course the chapel, is the north-west wing built by James V.

This remains much as it was, except that the interior was remodelled in the reign of Charles I and the windows enlarged when the palace was remodelled in the seventeenth century. The fine armorial panels have within the last few years been restored to their places. The rest of the palace, including the wing which corresponds to James V's building, belongs to a later period, but for convenience we will say the little we have to say about it here. It was designed for Charles II by Sir William Bruce of Kinross and built by Robert Mylne, the king's master mason. The plan is simple and stately. The series of staterooms on the first floor face east in the Hampton Court manner and have remarkably fine plaster ceilings. The great gallery has recently been the subject of some discussion. It is a somewhat ungainly room and the walls are lined with wretched portraits, for the most part imaginary, of the Scots kings. De Witt was commissioned to paint them, but judging from some charming chimney-piece panels from his brush in other rooms it is difficult to believe that the portraits in the gallery are his own work. The arrangement and framing are undoubtedly the work of Sir William Bruce. It was in this gallery that Prince Charles Edward's

HOLYROODHOUSE

INNES HOUSE, NEAR ELGIN

HALL OF FALKLAND PALACE

famous ball took place. The room has the air of never having been properly finished. A good floor and a good ceiling in keeping with the fine cornice would greatly improve it. So would the repainting of the woodwork with a less gloomy colour.

The noble remains of the Palace of Dunfermline have been described above (page 33).

From now onwards the absence of brick in Scotland constitutes a marked difference between its buildings and those of England. We have no Tattershall or Hurstmonceau or Thornton Abbey, no Hatfield or Bramshill, no Hampton Court, no Osterley. It is also worth noting that the E plan, so popular south of the Tweed ever since the Middle Ages, never occurs in Scotland before the seventeenth century and even then very rarely.

CHAPTER X

CASTLES—FOURTH PERIOD
1550–1700

We saw in the last chapter how a distinctively Scots style was evolved in the towers, courtyard castles and palaces of the fifteenth and early sixteenth centuries, and how renaissance ornament had after the year 1500 begun to replace Gothic in the more important buildings. In the period we have now to consider we shall see how the national style underwent further development. Advance in architecture—except perhaps in our own self-conscious day—occurs in response to changes in demand. Two such changes now occurred. With the passing of the monastic lands to the nobles and lairds at the Reformation it became possible for many families to live more comfortably than they had hitherto done and though Queen Mary's long minority and troubled reign were not propitious for building, the calm years which followed James VI's accession to the throne of England in 1603 saw the re-erection or

164

DUNDERAVE CASTLE

ARGYLL'S LODGING, STIRLING

enlargement of many of their houses. Meanwhile
—and this was the other change—defence was no
longer the first object. When gunpowder came
into general use about the middle of the fifteenth
century, it soon became evident that no stone
castle of the old type could stand a regular siege.
It was still necessary to have a house capable of
being secured at night and strong enough to ward
off a sudden attack. But in war the advantage
which had hitherto been with the defence had
passed to the attack. The defensive features,
hitherto so important, became obsolete. They
were not shorn off. They were retained, mainly
perhaps because everyone was accustomed to
them. In a treeless country, as most of Scotland
then was, the parapet walks and turrets may well
have had other than military uses. Their honourable history and undoubted beauty of form no
doubt appealed to the nice taste of the day. The
Scots were never a nation of artists, but, judged by
their buildings, it is certain that they were anything but careless. No doubt those who had to
build set about it in a business-like manner, like
the wiser of their descendants to-day, determined
to get the best that was going. The old defensive
features were not only retained, but modified to

meet new uses. The outcome was one of the most romantic and intensely national styles that the world has yet seen. The idea that the Scots architecture of this period was borrowed from France dies very hard. Billings seems to have been responsible for starting this hare. It is true, as we have seen, that certain ecclesiastical details were derived from the French flamboyant churches. It is also true that the builder of the staircase at Fyvie had probably seen the staircase at Blois and that there is some resemblance in the corbelling used for the support of turrets and chamfered corners. In the castles there was otherwise little resemblance except that they were derived from a thirteenth-century type common to both countries, and that in both certain defensive features were retained as ornaments after they had ceased to be required for military purposes. These had ceased to be used in France before the Scots style reached its full development—before such buildings as Craigievar or Glamis had been begun. The octagonal turrets so common in France are rare in Scotland. The square tower with acutely pointed roof which forms so conspicuous a feature in French castellated architecture is altogether unknown.

GLAMIS CASTLE

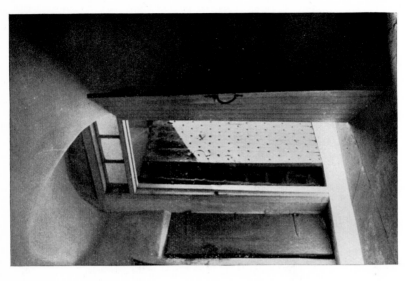

COXTON TOWER,
OLD DOOR AND YETT

AMISFIELD TOWER

So are the very tall dormers. In planning, which is the essence of building, there was never any resemblance between the two countries after the thirteenth century. The mouldings and ornaments are also quite different. But there is no need for further argument. Can anyone point to any French building which would look at home in Scotland or any Scots building which could possibly be mistaken for a French one?

The most characteristic castles of the period follow the tower plan and vary from simple square towers, like those of Coxton or Amisfield, to massive and elaborate piles like Craigievar or Castle Fraser. The reader will learn to distinguish the early from the later towers by the gradual change from military to domestic purposes. The walls, very thick in the earlier towers, tend to become thinner. The corbels on which the parapet rests become more elaborate and less severely practical. Shot holes go through the evolution described in the last chapter. After 1550 the parapet walk will be found in various stages of elimination till a hundred years later the roof completely covers the battlements and dormer windows are introduced, as in an ordinary house, to light the attic story. He will notice how the newel stairs, at first enclosed in the thick walls, tend to become wider as the walls grow thinner and are corbelled out beyond the face of the walls. Later, when separate communication to every room becomes an object, he will find these subsidiary stair turrets starting nearer and nearer the ground. He will notice how the angle turrets on the battlements, which began as open rounds, become more spacious when roofed in and used as separate rooms and how they are eventually extended downwards to provide similar rooms on the lower floors. Finally ogee roofs and balustrades indicate that the end of the seventeenth century is near. Design in Scotland was so conservative and varied so much with the locality that all these indicators must be used with caution. The student must also remember that the upper stages of many towers were remodelled long after they were built. An extension upwards, however inconvenient, was often, for the tower dweller, the cheapest way of increasing his accommodation. PRESTON TOWER (67) in Midlothian may serve as an example.

Let us take the smaller towers first. Late examples have been chosen to show how the tower persisted in Scotland after most of the great Tudor and Jacobean mansions had been erected, and even after Inigo Jones in the Queen's House at Greenwich had set the model for the classical country house. SMAILHOLM TOWER (1) has battlements on each side, but not at the gable ends. COXTON TOWER (67, 81) near Elgin is very small, about twenty-five feet square, with walls five feet thick. Though not built till 1644, it retains many features of the earlier towers. It consists of four vaulted rooms one above the other. The lowest with a door of its own seems to have been used as a store. The door to the hall is approached by an outside stair and defended by a yett immediately inside the door. The door is constructed of boards in the Scots manner, as described on page 217. The upper rooms are reached by a narrow turnpike stair in the thickness of the wall. The top story has turrets at three corners. Two are circular and are roofed in. The third is square and forms an open gallery with a door to the upper room. This is the only remnant of the battlement walk. The main roof is supported by a vault and covered with stone slabs, as are the roofs of the circular turrets. This is one of the few towers constructed entirely of stone. It has undergone so little alteration that it well deserves a visit which the courtesy of the owner renders easy. AMISFIELD TOWER (81) in Dumfriesshire is also quite small, measuring about thirty feet square, and consists of four rooms one above the other. The entrance is on the ground floor. The main stair is contained in a circular turret corbelled out from near the ground and again corbelled out to a square shape in the upper story. Here the battlements have entirely disappeared and the corner turrets are all roofed in. A turret perched on the gable supplies a place of look-out. The design of this tower with its plain walls below and very complicated top story is characteristic of this late phase.

We have seen how the tower in the last period was extended by the addition of a wing containing the staircase or additional rooms. The use of this form, which is known as the L plan, now became very general. MAYBOLE CASTLE (82), the house of the Earls of Cassillis in the town of Maybole, is a good example of this plan. It is remarkable for the charming oriel window in the top story of the staircase projection. Scotstarvet Tower in Fife is another well-preserved example, built in 1627—a gaunt formidable

82   MAYBOLE CASTLE, AYRSHIRE

CRAIGIEVAR CASTLE

looking tower, very carefully built, but giving little indication of its date except in the fanciful moulding of its parapet. Very often the stair was placed in a turret in the re-entering angle and the wing devoted to additional rooms. DUNDERAVE CASTLE (78) on the shore of Loch Fyne exemplifies the treatment. This charming building, long roofless, was restored with scrupulous care by Sir Robert Lorimer. The additions which were required to adapt it to present-day life are a model for such work, being kept strictly subservient to the old tower.

For the finest examples of this final phase of tower building we must look to the counties of Aberdeen and Angus. At CRAIGIEVAR (83) in Aberdeenshire this type of tower may be seen on the grand scale and in its full exuberance with turrets at every angle of the upper stories. On the only flat roof balusters have supplanted battlements and the highest turrets have ogee roofs which did not come into vogue till the seventeenth century. This superb example of the Scots tower was begun in 1610 and finished in 1624. It is happily well preserved and has even retained the ancient arrangement of the hall with its screens. The castle of Crathes in the same neighbourhood is almost equally fine and notable for the woodwork of its gallery on the top floor and two painted ceilings. The famous castle of GLAMIS (80) in Angus is perhaps the crowning example of this style, but here the turrets and dormers and the great circular staircase in the re-entering angle were superimposed on an older tower. Great ingenuity was employed here in the design of the roof, the centre of which is flat, forming an L-shaped walk enclosed with iron railings of the period. The gables are completely eliminated and replaced by square towers with balustrades and open turrets which form the ends of this airy terrace.

Sometimes a second wing was added at the diagonally opposite corner. This has been called the Z plan. These wings were placed so that they commanded the four walls of the main block. This may have been the original object, but the lighting of the principal rooms was probably also a consideration, as well as picturesque effect. This plan is well illustrated in the quaint castle of Claypotts which belongs to the city of Dundee and is well looked after by H.M. Office of Works. At Castle Fraser in Aberdeenshire the same design is followed on a much larger scale with all the

HUNTLY CASTLE

PEFFERMILL HOUSE

exuberance of Craigievar. At HUNTLY CASTLE (84) in the same county the elaboration of the top story is enhanced by a row of bow windows and bands of boldly carved inscriptions.

While these very ornate towers were being built in the north-east of Scotland, a new and more severe type of house was being evolved in Fife and the southern counties. PEFFERMILL (85) near Edinburgh is of this type. Here the L shape is retained, but the defensive features have entirely disappeared, though the newel staircase is still placed in a circular turret in the re-entering angle, where it can communicate directly with most of the principal rooms. At INNES (77) in Morayshire the staircase tower is in the same position but square and larger. Its broad flights of steps with landings at every corner lead easily to the upper rooms. The design was made by William Aytoun who had charge of the completion of Heriot's Hospital. In the details there is a close resemblance between the two buildings. In both the ornaments and mouldings are of a renaissance type very popular in Scotland during the seventeenth century and probably derived from contemporary work in Holland and Germany. They do not form an integral part of the design and are applied to uses of which the ancients never dreamed, being thus imbued with the nationality of the borrower. We shall see more of them later in this chapter. Peffermill was built in 1636 and Innes between 1640 and 1653. Both are comfortable houses and only needed bathrooms to bring them up to modern standards. Both are fortunately in good hands.

CASTLE STEWART (86) near Inverness illustrates very clearly the transition from castle to house. To the main block two subsidiary towers are attached, but instead of being placed diagonally, both are attached to the front, making it symmetrical in plan, though one of the towers is carried higher than the other and finished with a flat roof. This tower contains the door and a wide stair leading to the first floor. The door in the centre of the front is not part of the original design. The fenestration of this house is particularly interesting. The ground floor is devoted to cellars and offices which have small but adequate windows. The windows of the upper stories, though larger, are still small in relation to the spaces of bare wall. Yet all the rooms are admirably lighted and convince one that in modern houses the windows are often much too large for

CASTLE STEWART

Above: View from North-east

Below: Roof and Dormer Windows

TOLQUHON CASTLE

the rooms. Including the attic and basement
there are five stories. Large square corner
turrets at the back of the main block provide
additional rooms on the two top stories. This
building has all the appearance of a castle with
the accommodation of a large house and so much
convenience as is possible in the absence of
passages.

While most of the castles of this period followed
the tower plan, others assumed the more convenient form of ranges of building enclosing a
courtyard. There was nothing new in this plan.
It was derived from examples such as Craigmillar
or Crichton, where old towers had become embedded in a mass of additions, or others like
Doune where the courtyard plan had been
adopted from the outset.

TOLQUHON CASTLE (87) in Aberdeenshire was
so designed. It bears the following useful in-
scription : 'Al this wark excep the Auld Tour
was begun be William Forbes 15 April 1584 and
endit be him 20 October 1589.' The entrance
between two rounded towers with grated windows and a bold armorial panel resembles that of
Falkland on a small scale and forms a fine centre
in a front bounded by bold angle towers, one

round and one square. The court is surrounded by buildings on all four sides. The hall on the first floor opposite the gate is approached by a door in the corner of the court and entered from the landing of a spacious square staircase. A door at the other end of the landing leads to a long room with windows on three sides. This must have been the drawing room. Beyond it is a private room in the angle tower and at right angles to the latter a long narrow gallery over the entrance gate. The other buildings are unfortunately ruinous, but enough is left to show that this was a roomy and comfortable house. Below the hall a narrow passage leads from the main door to the kitchen with cellars leading off it, a great advance on most plans of this date. It is curious that the idea of a passage was so slow to assert itself. In this passage there is a semi-circular recess below the staircase fitted with a stone seat and intended apparently for a resting place for retainers. This interesting and very picturesque building has recently been put into excellent order by H.M. Office of Works.

FYVIE CASTLE (88) is a more magnificent example of the same type, though here only two sides of the court are enclosed by buildings. The

south front with its flanking towers is a work of
the fifteenth and sixteenth centuries, but it was
transformed in the early years of the seventeenth
century by Alexander Seton, Earl of Dunfermline, who added the top stories and turrets of the
flanking towers and the twin towers in the centre
with their imposing bridged top. This elevation,
the reader will observe, is the first in which we
have so far encountered a perfectly symmetrical
composition on a large scale. Whether it is improved by its rigid symmetry may be doubted.
At Tolquhon the design is well balanced, but
not symmetrical. Despite its modest scale it
seems more alive and more in keeping with the
tradition to which it belongs. Lord Dunfermline's work at Fyvie includes a remarkable circular staircase which leads to the principal rooms.
The space in which it is contained is about
twenty feet square and the newel from which the
steps radiate is one foot nine inches in diameter.
From this newel also radiate arches which support the vaults on which the steps rest. This
avoided the necessity for constructing the steps of
single stones. Their size would have made this
difficult, as some are ten feet long and the average
tread at the wall is thirty-two inches. The only

other circular stone staircases on this scale in Scotland are at Glamis and in the ruined castle of Noltland in Orkney. A few years after the completion of Fyvie Lord Dunfermline had occasion to remodel and enlarge PINKIE HOUSE (88) in Midlothian. Here he showed the same taste for long ranges of buildings and for marking the salient corners by turrets, but he refrained from repeating the oppressive symmetry of Fyvie. The long east front, before the roof was raised, must have been a very dignified composition with its seven tall chimneys and eight dormer windows. These are all of one pattern, but there is no attempt to mark the centre or make the design symmetrical. Three very successful new features were introduced, the long gallery on the top floor with its remarkable painted ceiling, its fine bow window facing south of a type not hitherto seen in Scotland and the very beautiful well head in the courtyard, the work of William Wallace, a noted sculptor.

Cawdor Castle is more compactly planned. Extensive buildings of this period surround an older tower built in 1454. The whole castle, including the top story of the tower, was remodelled about the middle of the seventeenth century. Low buildings projecting from the

88   Above: PINKIE HOUSE
Below: FYVIE CASTLE

89   STOBHALL

Above: The Terrace

Below: The Dower House

central tower divide the courtyard into three. This arrangement, unusual in Scotland, imparts, to what would otherwise be a fairly straightforward design, an air of mystery curiously appropriate to the grim history of the place.

It is impossible even to mention more than a few of the smaller buildings of this long and prolific period. STOBHALL (89) in Perthshire shows a group which no student should miss. This ancient home of the Drummonds, which still belongs to their descendant Lord Ancaster, stands delightfully on a steep bank above the Tay. It has always been well cared for and few buildings in Scotland are so little changed or so full of interest. The larger building consists of a tower with a chapel attached to it. This block dates from 1578. It has a porch with two doors giving north and south. An inner door defended by a sliding bar leads to a passage. This door is constructed on the method described above, and preserves its original studs. On the right is the chapel, oriented N.N.E., which retains the old altar slab under what ought to be the east window, the old Holy Water stoup, the ambry with its original door (52) and a most interesting painted ceiling which used to cut across the east window but has been altered to correct this fault but not spoilt. Above is a loft with a confessional constructed of wood in the simplest possible manner. The adherence of the Earls of Perth to the Catholic faith accounts for the survival of these fittings. In the seventeenth century Roman Catholic services were held here by special permission when forbidden elsewhere in Scotland. The approach to the chapel loft and the hall in the tower is by a newel stair, the rooms above it being reached by a smaller stair, which starts on the first floor. The whole house is in a wonderful state of preservation. The only room which has been substantially altered is one which was in an unhappy moment lined with pitch pine for Sir John Everett Millais, the painter, who lived there for a short time. None of the rooms are vaulted. At an angle to the tower, but separate from it, is a building which appears to have been a laundry with very low walls and a wide roof. Behind it again is the dower-house, built about 1650, with rooms on each side of the door, and, facing the entrance, a straight stair with moulded plaster ceiling. Attached to the dower house is the deep gateway by which the enclosure is entered, with a fine heraldic panel above the arch. The group

90   TRAQUHAIR, PEEBLESHIRE

From South-West
From North-East, with Terraces of 1695
The Closed Gates

HATTON HOUSE

Above: View from South-East

Below: Gateway

is completed by a building of cottage type which
contains the brewery and bakehouse. From the
enclosure, which is of irregular shape, the ground
falls rapidly on all sides but one. It is bounded
by terrace walls with low parapets over which the
river is seen far below. Outside the enclosure is
a garden and beyond that an avenue of old trees
leading up to the high road. All is kept in perfect order. This is a most pleasant spot, full of
peace and beauty, one of the rare places where
the work of man appears to be in perfect harmony
with nature.

At HATTON HOUSE (91), Midlothian, the additions made during this period to an older tower
form a compact block which comes very near the
type of country house which became popular in
the eighteenth century and has been repeated
with variations ever since. This was the work of
the unscrupulous Charles Maitland, afterwards
third Earl of Lauderdale. It was carried out
between 1664 and 1675 while he was Master of
the Mint and he is suspected of using public
money to pay for it. From his mother, who was
the daughter of Chancellor Seton, he seems to
have inherited the architectural sense of the
builder of Fyvie and Pinkie. Whoever made it,

the Hatton design has great merit. The entrance door faces a large courtyard bounded on the south side by a terrace wall. The door is in the centre of a low block, flanked on each side by taller wings to whose gables circular towers are attached at the outside corners. Behind the low block rises the old tower, still very grim despite the balustrade which has replaced its battlements and the graceful ogee roof which crowns its cape house. The front door opens into a spacious entrance hall leading on the left to a series of large and comfortable rooms looking south and on the right to a wide staircase by which a drawing-room over the entrance hall is approached. In this, the largest room in the house, the old idea of the hall seems to linger though stripped of all its medieval trappings. The original staircase was of stone and probably resembled the state staircase at Holyrood. It has, unfortunately, been replaced by a modern staircase.

The south elevation offers a delightful contrast to that facing the court. Both are bounded by circular towers, but on this side the ground falls away leaving room for a basement story and double flights of steps descending from the ground floor to a wide terrace and fountain. This

GALLERY, PINKIE HOUSE

Terrace

Sundial

ELLON CASTLE

front is narrower than the other as well as higher by the basement story. Further vertical emphasis is imparted to it by a central projection which is carried a story higher than the rest of the house. This projection is not in the true centre. There are three windows on one side and only two on the other, between it and the corner towers. The discrepancy is not disagreeable. Many people would never notice it, so effectually do the projection and corner towers engage the eye. The illusion is helped by the fact that the tower on the three window side is larger than the other. The lay-out round the house is on a noble scale and so carefully thought out that every part fits in neatly and logically with the others. The wide terrace above mentioned is supported by a high wall finished at each end with pavilions. In the centre below the terrace is a bathing pool enclosed in a grotto. Nearby there is a bowling green with a pavilion in which the original scoring boards remain—one with a cover which can be locked. The old approach to the courtyard was by a straight avenue between stone walls. At the far end was a gateway (91) which has been moved to a modern entrance lodge. At the other a flight of steps leads through another handsome gate to the courtyard. This place has been in good hands for many years, in none better than those of the present owner, who has restored much that in the past had been altered or allowed to fall into ruin. The walls of the house were originally covered with harling. The colour and texture of the rubble work revealed by its removal are so attractive that no one can regret the change.

Hatton has been described at length because it, and places like it, deserve careful study from the student of Scots architecture. Here we find all the comfort and much of the splendour of houses of the same period in England, but it is the work of Scots heads and Scots hands and in its broad lines, as well as in every detail, we are conscious of a national style. One cannot but deplore the loss of so fine a tradition. Can it be recaptured? While it lived it was common property. This means that the design was influenced, if you like limited, by what the builder was accustomed to produce and the patron to expect. These conditions can only be revived by a patient analytical study of which few minds are capable and the ability, scarcely less rare, to apply the results to the needs of to-day. Even so, success must depend on the existence of a more intelligent appreciation of architectural design than the present generation of Scotsmen seem to possess.

Quite as characteristic of Scotland, but in a different way, is the grim old Peeblesshire house of TRAQUHAIR (90). Here an ancient tower is embedded in a long barrack-like block of which one front gives on to a court enclosed between low wings, while the other looks down from high terraces bounded by pavilions, similar to those at Hatton. Why is this building so impressive? Probably because it is so plain, so utterly contemptuous of ornament and the niceties of symmetry. Its high roof, small windows, massive chimney and harled walls are intensely Scots, and viewing them one learns without surprise that Traquhair still declines to open its gates to any but a Stuart king.

DRUMLANRIG CASTLE (95) in Dumfriesshire and HERIOT'S HOSPITAL (95) in Edinburgh are the leading examples of a version of renaissance design quite different from that found in any other country. At Drumlanrig the broad lines of the house are admirably adapted to the beautiful and striking site and recapture most happily in symmetrical form the dignity of the ancient castle. Heriot's Hospital is a severe Scots version of the

English college with relatively low buildings enclosing a quadrangle. Both buildings have a definitely Scots character in the staircase turrets placed at the corners of the courtyards as well as in the corbelling and turrets of the main towers, though in both the gable which plays so important a part in the earlier buildings is completely eliminated. In both the detail is classical, but so remote in its application from anything Greek or Roman as to be almost barbaric. It captivates the fancy by its ingenuity and quaintness especially when rendered in the lovely rose-coloured freestone of the west. It is a thing to enjoy, but not to imitate without great caution. The late Sir Rowand Anderson, one of the few architects who really assimilated this style, made discreet use of it. Drumlanrig is one of the first houses in which passages formed an essential part of the original design. The formal approach to the hall or dining-room was from the open entrance loggia across the central court, but it could also be reached under cover by the passages. Like most buildings of this date Drumlanrig and Heriot's Hospital contain fine woodwork. This follows contemporary work in England much more closely than the stone work.

94 CULROSS, THE TOLBOOTH

95   Above: DRUMLANRIG CASTLE
Below: HERIOT'S HOSPITAL, EDINBURGH

The names of the men mainly responsible for these fine designs are not known. Heriot's Hospital was begun in 1618 and practically finished in 1650. Drumlanrig was not begun till about 1676 and finished in 1689. It is, therefore, unlikely that they were designed by the same man. Heriot's Hospital is known to have been finished by Aytoun, the builder of Innes. The design may have been made by Wallace who was employed as builder. It appears from the Duke of Buccleuch's papers that Sir William Bruce was consulted about the building at Drumlanrig and he appears to have been responsible for the upper stage of the tower of Heriot's Hospital which had been left unfinished.

ARGYLL'S LODGING, STIRLING (79), built in 1632, is the most important town house of this period. It has no passages except a short one on the ground floor, but four turret stairs give direct access to most of the rooms on its three floors, and there is another internal staircase from the hall to a large room on the first floor. The design is roughly symmetrical, but the correspondence of parts is not complete and most of the building is on the skew.

Along with the improvement in planning this

period witnessed a great advance in furnishing. Panelling succeeded hangings as a covering for the walls. Tables for various purposes, some with sliding leaves, others with folding tops and legs, came into use. So did cabinets for papers and books. Stools gave place to sets of chairs with cushions and upholstery and in the larger houses the sets included couches or day beds with folding backs which could be adjusted to any level. Furniture was still moved a good deal from house to house and the smaller cabinets were often fitted with iron handles by which they could be carried. Some of these, made of oak and yew with a sparing use of ebony, were probably made in Scotland. The larger frames with inlaid panels and carved heads and a more lavish use of ebony were probably imported.

In this period the architect's skill began to be applied to many other purposes besides churches and private houses. The old College in Glasgow, barbarously demolished in the nineteenth century, was second only to Heriot's Hospital in importance. Cowane's Hospital, Stirling, is a smaller but carefully designed building. The sturdy and widely spaced balusters of its terrace are characteristic of the time. Many tollbooths were now

INVERKEITHING

TAIN

TOLBOOTHS

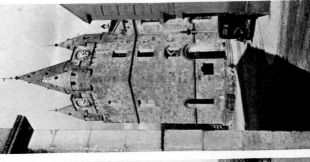

STIRLING

MERCAT CROSS,
INVERKEITHING

MERCAT CROSS,
ABERDEEN

97

built. Most of those in the southern counties
have been altered but good examples survive at
TAIN and STIRLING (96), and CULROSS (94). The
smaller houses and cottages of the period have
for the most part been demolished or changed
beyond recognition, but at Culross in Fife
enough is left to show what a small Scots town
was like. The National Trust has already done
much to preserve this intensely interesting place
and it is to be hoped it will receive sufficient support to render its work complete. Apart from
buildings, many fine and characteristic works of
architect and sculptor have survived. Of MERCAT
CROSSES (97) that at Aberdeen, erected in 1686,
is the finest, but others of elegant design are
found at Preston, Kincardine-on-Forth, Doune,
Airth and Inverkeithing. The last is probably
the oldest, and is believed to date from the early
fifteenth century. The well head at Pinkie has
already been noticed. The fountain at Ravelston
is of a type rare in Scotland. The SUNDIALS at
ELLON (93), Newbattle, MELVILLE HOUSE (99)
and Alloa are good specimens of a feature which
has always had a special attraction for Scotsmen.

CHAPTER XI

BUILDING AFTER 1700

We have seen that in the late seventeenth century the accommodation in houses and public buildings was very much what it is to-day, though people were still content to reach one room through another. The transition to the kind of planning which held its own all through the eighteenth century and most of the nineteenth occurred very suddenly in Scotland, a few years before 1700. It appears to have been mainly due to the influence of Sir William Bruce of Kinross, who died in 1710. Bruce was reared in the old tradition and his early works, such as the Steeple of the old Merchant's Hall in Glasgow (5) or the gateways at Pollok Castle (98) which are attributed to him, are as fine as anything the seventeenth century produced. His later domestic work shows close acquaintance with the designs of Wren and his contemporaries in England. He is credited by tradition with the design of three large houses which are quite

98   Above: POLLOKSHAWS BURGH HALL
      Below: POLLOK CASTLE, GATEWAY AND PAVILION

MELVILLE HOUSE, LADYBANK

modern in the sense that all medieval trappings have been discarded, that there is convenient access to every room and that the arrangements and decoration are perfectly suited to the life of to-day. The houses in question are his own house at Kinross, built in 1685, Moncrieff House in Perthshire and MELVILLE HOUSE (99) in Fife, built in 1692 for the first Earl of Melville. For the designs of the first two he is believed to have been personally responsible, as he certainly had been for the building at Holyrood, completed in 1679. At Melville he was probably only an adviser, as the house is recorded to have been designed by Mr. James Smith, afterwards supervisor of the Royal Castles and Palaces in Scotland. All these houses have the traditional Scots merit of thick walls, good chimneys and reasonable scale, but their design represents a complete revulsion from the elaborate castellated style still practised at that time in the northern counties. It shows an ingenuity in planning not hitherto seen north of the Tweed. Among other devices, that of the mezzanine story is most happily used, so happily that it makes it quite easy to modernize the house. At Melville the internal fittings bear evidence of a businesslike determination on the part of the owner to have nothing but the best. The oak panelling, leather work and furniture, as well as the tapestries and velvets of the state rooms, are as fine as anything at Hampton Court or Chatsworth and as good to-day as when the house was finished two hundred and forty-five years ago. None of these except the panelling were made in Scotland. The house is large, but no house could be more compact or more comfortable. In summer it is deliciously cool, in winter so warm that a rudimentary stove below the great staircase supplies all the central heating required. On such perfection there can be little advance, and in fact there has been none except in the matter of bathrooms and lifts. Though the house stands under a hill its chimneys have never been disgraced by a chimney pot. This can be said of few buildings except those of Wren, whose Chelsea Hospital is, in this respect, such a contrast to its neighbours in London.

The house at Melville was harled, the windows and doors being surrounded by fine bolection mouldings in dressed stone. The basement story is treated as a plinth marked by a bold stone moulding and there is a stone cornice below the eaves. The harling has been removed on three sides of the house, revealing rubble work of pleasant texture and colour. The lay-out is simple but dignified. At the back, to which the main entrance was moved a hundred years ago, the house abuts directly on the park. In front there is a large courtyard now converted into a garden. It has low wings on each side containing offices. A curved flight of steps ascends to the old front door. Opposite the door there is a gate with massive pillars and lead statues, and at the corners spacious pavilions with ogee roofs which seem to have served as coach houses. The house is approached by a splendid avenue of beeches. Seen over the gate and between the pavilions it looks very tall and stately. This is not unlike the lay-out at Hatton, though less elaborate, and closely resembles that at Pollok Castle, which is attributed to Bruce himself.

Bruce's mantle descended on William Adam (1689-1748) who had worked for him and completed the great house at Hopetoun which he had begun. DUMFRIES HOUSE (100), Ayrshire, built by Adam for an ancestor of Lord Bute, is one of the finest and least spoilt of his numerous country houses. He employed an admirable plasterer, named Clayton, who decorated two noble rooms at Blair Atholl, and whose stucco work can be traced by the use of the same moulds at Oxenfoord and Nether Pollok. The fine furniture found in large houses of this date seems all to have been purchased from English makers. At Blair Castle the accounts are still preserved. Of William Adam's public buildings, the Town House of Dundee was perhaps the best known and most valued by all except Dundonians. It was demolished in 1931 by the Dundee Corporation. After his death in 1748 his four gifted sons carried on building all over Great Britain till the close of the eighteenth century. Their work was less massive than their father's but richer in fancy and grace. The new REGISTER HOUSE in Edinburgh (101) is theirs. It has the exquisite proportion of their best work without a trace of the pretentiousness which sometimes marred it. The north side of Charlotte Square is another fine example. St. George's Church, on the west of the Square which closes the vista of George Street, is the work of Robert Reid (1776-1856) who also designed the buildings in Parliament Square. It was built in 1811. Its dome, set well forward over the entrance, is of great beauty and

DUMFRIES HOUSE, AYRSHIRE

EDINBURGH

Above: High School

Below: New Register House

nicely adjusted in scale to the long wide street which it faces. The lay-out of the new town in Edinburgh, of which this square is an early instalment, dates from the last years of the eighteenth century. It shows how far sighted the improvers of this time were and how determined to produce something perfect and durable. The houses are not only of high quality, both in design and workmanship, but are marked by a practical good sense which has prevented them from becoming old fashioned, except to those who judge everything by its novelty, and has endeared them to those who live in them. The Adam brothers, who in the classical jargon of the time liked to be called the Adelphi, were succeeded by Archibald Elliot, the designer of the bold lay-out which links up Princes Street with the Calton Hill, including the Regent Bridge. In the next generation Roman models were superseded by Greek. The Neo Greek ideals were pressed to their utmost limits by Thomas Hamilton (1785-1858) who built the Edinburgh HIGH SCHOOL (101) and its near neighbour the Burns Monument, and William Henry Playfair (1789-1857) who designed the two buildings on the Mound and the terraces on the

Calton Hill. These men earned for Edinburgh its appellation of the modern Athens.

The American War of Independence deprived Glasgow of the tobacco trade, but cotton came to the rescue. David Hamilton (1768-1843) carried out many important works in Glasgow and its neighbourhood, among them the Royal Exchange, HUTCHESONS' HOSPITAL (112), the Western Club and Hamilton Palace. When the last was demolished, the paving stones from the vast basement were cut up and used to pave the choir of Paisley Abbey, a transfer which may puzzle the antiquary of the future. Another architect of note in Glasgow was Alexander Thomson (1817-1875), better known as Greek Thomson, whose designs in recent years have excited a great deal of interest in this and other countries. St. Vincent's Church and the terraces in Great Western Road are good examples of his peculiar style. The work of this group was part of the movement which produced the Madeleine in Paris, the British Museum in London and St. George's Hall in Liverpool. Their work in Scotland suffers a good deal from the material in which it was carried out and from the dirt which has dulled it down. Designs so severe demand pleasing materials, especially when the buildings are on a small scale. Had Portland stone been available or a rosy sand stone, their beauty of proportion would have been more evident, whereas in a cold grey stone blackened by smoke they look gloomy and out of place. But these buildings are still in the awkward age. Possibly the weathering of another century may make them more interesting. Even so, a style which is so much afraid of windows can never be really at home in our climate.

Aberdeen, apart from the distinction which the use of granite gives any city, contains some notable modern buildings. The early years of the last century produced many of those classical designs to which this intractable material lends itself so well. Archibald Simpson, who designed the North of Scotland Bank among many other works, and Thomas Mackenzie, set the key of this movement. But it is to the brilliant son of the latter, Alexander Marshall Mackenzie (1848-1933) that the city owes its most remarkable buildings. He inherited a double gift of design, for his maternal grandfather, William Marshall, famous for his reels and strathspeys, was responsible for many improvements on the Gordon Estates. This versatile architect worked in many styles, but through all his designs there runs the same concentrated vigour, as if he had decided from the outset exactly what impression he intended his work to make and brushed aside everything which did not contribute to that impression. The new buildings at MARISCHAL COLLEGE (102), a work of his middle life, are based, like all good work, on tradition, but not fettered by it. The writer had the good luck to see them first on a winter morning when the sun was breaking through a snowstorm and the delicate tracery of parapets and spires were outlined in silver against a blue sky. They seemed, and still seem, to him a perfect expression of granite design as practised in the best buildings of Brittany, Wales or Cornwall. Those who contrast with disapproval the severity of the three stories of class rooms and offices with the airy lacework of the parapets and pinnacles, do not grasp the nature of this imperishable rock, so unsuitable for the ornament we are accustomed to see wrought in freestone, but capable of daring uses in which the hardest freestone would have but a short life. In this building the architect, taking a hint from St. Pol de Léon but working

ABERDEEN, NEW BUILDINGS

Above: At Marischal College

Below: At King's College

MURTHLY, NEW CASTLE

ABERDEEN, GRANITE VILLA

on a much larger scale, has happily combined the cyclopean with the gossamer.

In the new buildings at KING'S COLLEGE (102), Old Aberdeen, Marshall Mackenzie's object was quite different. He sought to follow the scale and traditional forms of the older buildings and create that collegiate atmosphere which is the soul of Oxford and Cambridge, but so conspicuously absent in Scotland since the old Glasgow College was destroyed.

In the outskirts of Aberdeen there are many charming houses built of granite dating from 1800 onwards. Seen among trees, with the glistening pillars and crisp shadows of their porticoes, they seem to strike just the right note for a suburban villa (103).

Among nineteenth century architects Gillespie Graham (1777?-1855) has had less honour than he deserves. It is said that A. W. Pugin, whom he befriended when shipwrecked in the Forth, helped him with the design of the spire of the Assembly Hall which is such an outstanding feature of the Castle Hill. The design has also been claimed for Thomas Hamilton. It bears so little resemblance to the work of either that it is more probably his own. The design for the new castle at MURTHLY (103) in Perthshire was certainly his own. Based on Jacobean models, this unfinished house, for dignity, proportion and beauty stood quite alone in its day and is still without a rival.

Church building, outside the larger towns, has not been of much interest since 1700. The homely white-washed churches which continued the pre-reformation tradition in the Highlands have already been noticed. The Lowland churches of the same period were larger and galleries were a prominent feature. Till the end of the eighteenth century they were severely plain with classical details, and occasionally a steeple in the Wren manner, with a dismal bell. Early in the nineteenth century a good many parish churches were rebuilt in a sort of Tudor Gothic which had nothing Scots about it except the sensible arrangement of the interior and a stern determination not to look pretty. The parish churches of Doune and Larbert are two of many, all very much alike. In recent years many attempts have been made to humanize these gaunt buildings. At Bothwell, as we have seen, the object was to marry the new church to the old collegiate chancel. It was happily achieved by removing the galleries and the plaster. At Kippen, the plan has been to add things of beauty. In both cases, the nineteenth century structure has been treated with respect, without any attempt to disguise it or introduce incongruous features. Had the old structures been made to look silly and old fashioned, as they easily might have been, the harmony which now delights all comers would not have been there. Only in out of the way places, where local talent had a chance, does one find churches of this date with any individuality (104).

The outburst of church building which followed the Disruption was handicapped by the need of making the greatest show with the least expenditure. In the last fifty years many good churches have been built, but without much regard for Scots tradition, except in the work of the late Dr. Macgregor Chalmers, who ingeniously harnessed to modern uses the simple type of romanesque used by the early Celtic builders.

In recent years Scotland has had its share of the various phases of modern construction, including steel frames and ferro concrete. Many fine buildings have risen and others of which we have less reason to be proud, but none has the slightest national flavour. For an attempt to keep alive the national style, which is the subject of this book, we must look back to the first half of the nineteenth century.

The Scottish Baronial revival will always be associated with the name of William Burn (1789-1870) who practised in Scotland till 1844 when he removed to London, leaving his Edinburgh practice to his partner David Bryce (1803-1876). These two men were the fashionable architects of their day and it was a long one. Both were reared in the classical style and the Gothic as understood in their day—Burn built the Church of St. John at the west end of Princes Street, and Bryce, the Bank of Scotland above the Mound. Between them they built a very large number of country houses great and small. The romantic ideals which had inspired the incoherent design of Abbotsford, had by Scott's genius been spread far and wide. It was, no doubt, in response to this impulse that Burn turned his attention to the castellated architecture of his own country. Under its rather pretentious name, the revival caught on in a way which it is now difficult to understand. The flame was fanned by the publication of Robert Billings'

EDDERTON

FOCHABERS

DAVIOT

CULROSS, FIFE.   THE STUDY AND THE CROSS

Baronial and Ecclesiastical Antiquities, with its beautiful steel engravings—really steel-faced etchings—which began to appear in 1845. It is a pity that this revival produced such poor stuff, the more so as much good eighteenth century work was swept away to make room for it. One has only to look at its heavy crowsteps and thin chimneys to realize that the new was a most unscholarly imitation of the old. Its strong point was its comfortable planning, its main defect the attempt to combine large plate glass windows with medieval fortifications imperfectly understood. When, as occasionally happened, the patron insisted on a design in the classical or Jacobean manner, Burn could be relied on to produce a very comfortable and convenient, though rather ugly, house. Bryce was less successful in this respect. Too many of his rooms were spoilt by useless turrets and there is a tiresome sameness about his designs. Only in subsidiary buildings where the form was dominated by the purpose did he catch something of the true Scots spirit.

Later in the century, Sir Rowand Anderson (1834-1921) played a leading part both as architect and teacher. In the School of Applied Art, he was remarkably successful in arousing interest in old Scots buildings. Many of the ablest architects of yesterday and to-day were trained in his office. His restorations at Jedburgh, Dunblane and Paisley showed a great advance on anything hitherto attempted in that line. He practised at first in partnership with Hew Montgomerie Wardrop (1856-1887) who was a bolder Bryce. Sir Rowand's own buildings covered a wide field. His first work on his own was the completion of Beaufort Castle after Wardrop's death. This large house showed more scholarship and a better grasp of Scots design than any work of Burn or Bryce. A devastating fire has recently revealed the excellence of its construction. Notable among his works are the noble dome of the Edinburgh University and the McEwan Hall, and, in another vein, the Pearce Institute, Govan, and BURGH HALL of POLLOKSHAWS (98), where he deliberately set out to save from oblivion some of the fine features of the old Glasgow College. This he contrived to do without any sacrifice of the purpose of the building. Sir Rowand was not always happy in his choice of materials. The red sandstone pillars of the McEwan Hall never look comfortable. The brick linings of his stone churches at Govan and Inchinnan appear harsh and common. The red tile roof of a house which he built for Lord Strathcona in Glencoe was so glaringly foreign that the tiles have since been replaced by slates from the neighbouring quarry of Ballachulish. These were more the faults of the period than of the man. His response to beauty was quick and sincere. He was one of the first modern architects to understand and practise the delicately blended style which bloomed for a moment when Gothic was invaded by the first hint of the Renaissance. The house he built for himself at Colinton in the seventies—a small house with two really good rooms approached by an ample staircase and corridor—shows the admirable use which can be made of traditional form by a man of independent mind and the dignity which can be imparted to a small building by judicious planning.

There was a fine reserve about Sir Rowand's work. Enough, but never too much was his motto. He liked buildings above all to look apt for their purpose. The writer with the impertinence of youth once asked him what he would do, if, after designing what he considered a fine room he were asked to spend more money on it. The answer was expected to turn on an oak floor, a rich ceiling, a noble frieze or perhaps carved doors and shutters. With a shake of the head and one of those cheerful sighs which his friends will remember, but without the slightest hesitation, he replied, 'I should make the walls thicker'.

Among the many distinguished architects trained in Anderson's office, Sir Robert Lorimer perhaps played the most important part in moulding the taste of his day. He was the first modern architect who thoroughly absorbed the old building traditions of his country. His works were in no sense copies. No one who examines them could possibly mistake them for old buildings. Sometimes, as at ARDKINGLAS (106), he even omitted such characteristic features as the gable chimneys. Yet his houses are so completely saturated with the spirit of the old builders and show so complete a mastery of their technique that those who come unexpectedly upon them for the first time, as one may do on the group at FORMAKIN (106) in Renfrewshire, are for the moment completely staggered, and where all is new, are left wondering how much is old. We have already discussed the difficulty of re-

106   Above: FORMAKIN, RENFREWSHIRE
Below: ARDKINGLAS, ARGYLL

SCOTTISH WAR MEMORIAL

turning to a lost tradition. Lorimer had precisely the gifts which make such a return possible. He recognized that the character of a building is not determined by form alone, that it lies even more, though less obviously, in texture, scale and silhouette, in the relation of part to part, the pitch of the roof, the subtle battering of walls, the pleasant irregularity which enlivens work done by hand and eye without mechanical guides. Though it added enormously to his labours, his attention to these vital factors never flagged.

His designs were dictated by the purpose of the building, so that his elevations grew naturally out of his plans, but he never accepted the view that every detail in architecture must have some functional significance. He was, on the contrary, always prepared to make some sacrifice of construction and even convenience, where sentiment or appearance required it. Once, when he was designing a small house, it was suggested that the housewife might find single sheets of plate glass easier to clean than sashes divided by astragals into several small panes. 'I realize that,' said he, 'but I don't see how any character can be put into a little house like this without astragals.' In saying so he faced up to a disagreeable fact

which many architects have shirked. He had the
secret of watching and guiding other people's
work without hindering or deadening it. He
never claimed credit for the craftsman's suc-
cesses. On the contrary, he gave full credit to
the craftsman, even where his own guidance had
been essential. It is perhaps from this ability to
inspire the craftsman that the quiet harmony and
completeness of his work springs. The Thistle
Chapel has already been described. This was
perhaps the only building in which he had a
perfectly free hand. It was also the most de-
liberate attempt he ever made to work in the
spirit of a bygone age.

In the NATIONAL WAR MEMORIAL (107) in Edinburgh Castle, on which he lavished all his resource
and energy, he had a large measure of freedom,
but his first and finest design for a great octagon
was rejected on account of the reluctance of his
fellow countrymen to accept any change in the
outline of the Castle rock. Though tenacious of
his own opinion, he always kept an open ear for
disinterested advice. When the octagon was
turned down, suggestions poured in on him and
the new design was actually based on some of
these. When the building was nearing com-

pletion, he toyed with the idea of crowning the gable of the shrine with an open lantern in which a light should burn day and night as a symbol of constancy. He asked a level-headed Scots woman what she thought of this idea. 'If it is to be a lamp which somebody tends,' was the reply, 'well and good, but if it is a case of laying on current from the company's main, no.' No more was heard of that proposal.

Lorimer, still learning, has gone, but happily in architecture, as in other fields, discoveries once made become common property. It is in the power of his successors, starting from the point where he left off, to carry his work far beyond the point he reached and harness to modern purposes all that is worth keeping of an ancient and honourable tradition. No one expects or desires mere copies of old buildings, but we do desire designs inspired by history and scholarship, designs in which a serious attempt is made to carry what has proved good a step nearer perfection. Such designs will bear to old Scots work the same relation that Liverpool Cathedral bears to the great churches of the Middle Ages.

CHAPTER XII

SMALL HOUSES, COTTAGES AND OTHER BUILDINGS

We have been concerned so far mainly with churches and castles and a few public buildings. We turn now to the smaller houses, more numerous but unfortunately less permanent, in which the bulk of the Scots race has been reared ; houses which at this moment are engaging the anxious attention of all who care for these precious records of the national life.

Early houses of this small type are more often found in towns than in the country. PROVAND'S LORDSHIP (3) in Glasgow has already been mentioned in connection with the Cathedral. It dates from the fifteenth century and is well worth a visit if it were only to see the seventeenth-century furniture collected there. This includes some fine chairs and several good specimens of the small cupboards—probably of native manufacture—in which our forebears kept their papers. PROVAN HALL (3), the country abode of the same Prebendary,

108 Above: COTTAGES AT LEUCHARS

Below: KIRKCALDY, OLD HOUSES IN SAILORS' WALK

109 HAMILTON DOWER HOUSE, PRESTONPANS
Below: Courtyard

is of the same date and is at this moment under-going restoration. In KIRKCALDY (108) there is a house on the Sailors' Walk which certainly goes back to 1660 and may be much older. It has suffered from subdivision and neglect but, luckier than most, has escaped serious alteration and is now being put in order for the National Trust, thanks to the generosity of a citizen of Kirkcaldy. The HAMILTON DOWER HOUSE (109) in Preston-pans, built in 1628, perhaps shows this type at its best. It surrounds three sides of a small courtyard and consists of a single story with attics above. The small scale of this house renders it a particu-larly valuable model. It is in a fair way to be saved by co-operation between the County Council and the National Trust. It shows how well the national style lends itself to the type of house required to-day. In all these houses ornament is used with a sparing hand, but in such a way as to give them great character. It is concentrated on gates, doorways and dormers and is usually very personal, consisting of coats of arms, initials, cyphers, inscriptions and dates. The heraldry and lettering are always of the best.

In the larger towns, and especially in Edin-burgh, there are a good many houses of this sort and size which were the town abodes of important families. Huntly House in the High Street, recently restored by the Edinburgh Corporation and used as a local museum, deserves a visit from everyone who wants to know what an old Edinburgh house was like. So does Aitchison House, its next door neighbour, which at the moment of writing is being privately and most conscientiously reconditioned. On a larger scale on the same side of the High Street is Moray House with its imposing gate, tall rooms and elaborate plaster ceilings of the early seventeenth century. This historic street, which stretches from Holyrood to the Castle, is undergoing numerous changes and no one can deny that many of its houses need reconditioning. Fortunately the city authorities are beginning to realize their value as a civic asset. The law and the health regulations conspire to render their preservation very difficult, but it is to be hoped that the old fronts at least will be kept. No modern imitation, however skilful, can have the same value as an authentic wall which has been in place two or three hundred years. In the centre of the larger towns, tenements from an early date took the place of cottages. In the capital the narrow-

110 Above: CAITHNESS FARM WITH FLAGSTONE FENCES
Below: LANARKSHIRE FARM

III · BALNACRAIG, ABERDEENSHIRE
Below: Garden Fence

ness of the ridge on which the old town is built led to the erection of very high tenements as early as the seventeenth century. They have been for three centuries as much a feature of Edinburgh as the skyscrapers are of New York and the same simplicity of design gives them the same kind of beauty. In Edinburgh it is much enhanced by the steep slope from which the blocks rise.

There were many small country houses half way in size between the cottage and the laird's house, inhabited by bonnet lairds, dowagers and professional men. Unfortunately most of these have disappeared or been altered beyond recognition. Those that remain are of great interest and precious to the architect who is employed to-day on building precisely the same type of house. The Dower House at Stobhall (89) is a good example. Another of rather later date is found at BALNACRAIG (111) in Aberdeenshire. Unfortunately its window sashes have been altered. It is remarkable for its attractive garden fence, consisting of a low wall with granite posts supporting a high wooden railing. Readers who know Spain will recall a more ambitious fence of the same type which encloses the Royal Gardens at Aranjuez. At Skellater on Donside there is a charming example which was built in 1770. Here a refinement long used in Aberdeenshire is employed with most telling effect. All the walls are built with a batter, not noticeable unless you look for it, but enough to give extraordinary dignity to a very simple design.

Between 1750 and 1850 a great deal of moorland was brought under the plough. The return was rapid and high and the increased revenue was used to establish and equip more farms. Nearly all the farms as we know them to-day were the creation of that period and in many the original buildings still survive (110). All the country buildings of this period were carefully designed and as carefully constructed. Some of the best brains of the day were at work on them. They had a literature of their own. They are solid, straightforward and never ostentatious. A desire for symmetry and fine proportion runs through the designs. Here and there a Classic or Gothic touch is added, but only by way of flavouring. Where burns were available water wheels were installed, otherwise the horse had to provide the motive power. The circular or octagonal sheds in which that patient beast turned the wheel are a picturesque adjunct of the carse farms. This period of carefully planned development is the Golden Age of Scotland. Every detail of these fruitful years repays study from the machinery for the removal of the mosses to the neat mahogany cupboard in which the laird kept his accounts and the plans of the new farms.

The drystone turf-thatched cottage (4) perpetuates in the Highlands a type which is certainly very ancient. One cannot regret that these primitive cabins are being replaced by better houses, so long as a few specimens are preserved. After mortar bound walls superseded those of dry stone, there was little change in the form of the typical lowland cottage, until it was superseded by the bungalow after the Great War. The traditional form must be familiar to every reader ; a rectangular building of one or two stories with gabled ends and walls of rubble, usually covered with harling ; a door in the middle of the front, with the stair opposite, if there is an upper story ; a room on each side with fireplaces in the gables ; a roof covered with flags, thatch, slates or tiles, with stone ridge and stout chimneys. The earlier houses have crowstepped gables and dormer windows. Sometimes the main gable faces the road or street (108). In the larger villages and small towns the houses are more ambitious. Some have projecting stair turrets, square or circular, and often the upper story is entered by an outside stair. These features, simple in themselves, are capable of producing the most charming combinations, as may be seen in many a village from Berwick right up to THURSO (115). Occasionally, as in Elgin, arcades ran below the houses, affording a sheltered walk for pedestrians, but only remnants of this attractive arrangement survive. After the seventeenth century, dormer windows became less common. Gables were finished with straight skews instead of crowsteps and, except in a few east coast villages, rarely faced the street. These later houses are built end to end, often forming a continuous line, with gables serving two houses. They were sometimes deep enough to have rooms facing to the back as well as the front. In the Clyde valley a central gable with one or two windows and a chimney became a common feature about 1800. When dormer windows were abandoned, the upper rooms were lit by windows below the eaves. For the sake of economy the ceilings of the upper rooms were carried into the roof and the windows were apt to be too low. As the nineteenth century advanced, this objection was met by the introduction of storm windows with splayed sides, like small bow windows. This pleasant feature, so characteristic of the Scots village, is only suitable for a fairly steep roof and appears sadly out of place in the low pitched roofs of the modern builder. The typical angle of a Scots roof up to the end of the seventeenth century was 55°, but after that the angle tended to grow wider.

The older doors were of the ordinary Scots type, made of boards nailed together without any frame. The upright boards on the outside were usually of oak studded with nails. The inner horizontal boards were often of pine. The door opened with a latch and there was sometimes a knocker or a tirling pin in the centre. The hinges were of iron, made by the local smith, simple but nearly always elegant. The lock was enclosed in a wooden case.

Till well on in the seventeenth century, the windows were glazed in the upper half, with wooden shutters below which opened on hinges, but this arrangement has almost everywhere been replaced by sash windows. In the smaller sash windows, the upper sash was usually a fixture, while the lower had neither cords nor weights, but was lifted by hand and supported by a hook. Casements would have been more convenient and more sanitary for small windows, but they have never been popular in Scotland. It seems at first sight strange that a form of window so universally employed in France should be almost unknown here. The explanation seems to be that the connection between the two countries had ceased to be intimate before casement windows became general in France, thanks to that excellent contrivance the Spanish bolt, which we use only for glazed doors leading to gardens or balconies. In the eighteenth century, great attention was paid to the details of windows. In the simple country cottage, the harling was carried into the window opening to meet the sash. In carefully finished houses, the windows had plain surrounds of dressed stone. Projecting sills did not come into use till after 1800. The favourite proportion for the opening was a height equal to double the width. With six panes to each sash this resulted in panes bearing in width to height, the pleasant golden proportion of five to eight. This may have been arrived at unconsciously, but no one can doubt that the builders had a firm grasp of the fact now too often neglected, that the design of a small house depends almost as much on its windows as the human face on its eyes and that the scale is set by the panes. This was probably one of the reasons why heavy astragals were used long after it must have been apparent that the construction did not require them. Where more light was needed in small houses the windows were sometimes grouped in pairs. After 1700 the additional light was obtained by adding narrower openings at each side of the main window. In such cases the pane was always the unit which governed the size of the openings. When these triple openings look awkward, as they often do in modern buildings, it is nearly always because this rule has been disregarded.

A note on the future of the Scots cottage may not be out of place here. But first we must observe that the industrial development of the nineteenth century did not, unfortunately, adopt the high standards set by the rural development on whose heels it followed. It was hasty and haphazard. It may have been supposed that the deposits of coal and iron on which the new prosperity depended would not last more than a generation. Nearly all the buildings were shoddy and bad—a warning to us who are building so hastily to-day. The one object was to get rich quick. Occasionally a factory was well designed, like that of Messrs. Coats at Paisley (112), erected in 1886, occasionally the workers were housed in well built cottages, but these were rare exceptions. That toleration of dirt and ugliness which still renders the industrial districts so depressing had begun. The standard had been definitely lowered. The landscape of the iron shanty, cinder road and dead tree, had become part of Scotland.

Until 1914, there was a marked difference between Scots and English cottages, so much so that a village in the south of England had not the slightest resemblance to a Scots village. In Wales and Northern England the difference was less, but the Scots house was decidedly more substantial.

Two years ago it looked as if most of the old cottages in Scotland would be swept away except when they were bought and reconditioned by people who wanted week-end houses. The Housing Act of 1935 allowed no grant for reconditioning unless the cottage was occupied by

112   Above: HUTCHESON'S HOSPITAL, GLASGOW
Below: MESSRS. COATS' FACTORY, PAISLEY

113   Above: HOUSES AT KIPPEN
Below: A HOUSE AT BIGGAR

an agricultural labourer and it paid the county councils better to demolish the old villages with their stone houses and transfer the population to new and often flimsy bungalows. Happily an arrangement has been made between the Ministry of Health and the Ancient Monuments Department, which should result in the preservation of houses of special interest. For the rest, the only hope lies in co-operation between public authorities, private persons and voluntary associations, such as the National Trust and the A.P.R.S., which stand for the preservation of amenities, historic as well as natural.

Local Authorities have often a difficult choice to make. The case of two cottages in the Stirlingshire village of KIPPEN (113) is a case in point. These cottages stand conspicuously at the end of the street and on them the old world character of the village—which is its fortune—largely depends. The cottages were purchased by the County Council some years ago, along with another now demolished, in order to widen the road which at this point curves rapidly down hill. The cottage already demolished projected on to the road and is certainly better out of the way. The others are open to the objection that their doors open directly on to the road. Most of the villagers desire to keep the cottages and suggest that they should be reconditioned, with access from the ends. The Highways Committee having bought the cottages for road widening has no intention of spending money on reconditioning them. How can this problem be solved? Only, so far as one can see, by the sale of the cottages to some private person or society who will recondition them in the way suggested. Would the County Council be justified in agreeing to sell them ? To any outsider it appears that they would. Their purpose in acquiring the cottages would seem to have been served by the demolition of one cottage and the alteration of the entrances to the others. Cottages are required in the village and the reconditioning of these would provide two without expense to the ratepayers, who would further benefit by the sale. The wish of the villagers would be met. There would therefore seem to be a good hope that the cottages may be saved.

In both countries there has been deterioration since the War, but it has been much greater north of the Tweed. The municipal building schemes which have played so important a part in recent

ELDERSLIE

DINGWALL

FALKLAND

THURSO

STRATHMIGLO, FIFE

development, have in England been for the most
part in the hands of experienced architects, and
some of the results achieved round London,
Liverpool and Manchester are strikingly good.
In Scotland the design of such schemes has
nearly always been left to over-worked officials
who have neither the leisure nor the training
necessary to give their work distinction. The
standard of design has fallen very low, and still
lower in the work of the speculative builder, who
never employs an architect except in the rare
cases where one of the firm has had some architectural training. The houses are usually comfortable whether built by municipal or private
enterprise, and full credit for this must be given
to all concerned. But the new settlements are by
general consent ugly and monotonous. This is
not surprising, since cheapness and haste have
been the first considerations. Ignorant attempts
to avoid monotony often make things worse, the
alternation, for instance, of tile and slate roofs,
sham black and white gables, or a higgledy-
piggledy lay-out which is neither symmetrical nor
picturesque and bears no reference to the site.
Stone as a building material for small houses has
for the last twenty years been almost abandoned

Ugliness has been stressed by the lack of good bricks north of the Tweed and by the absence of any attempt to keep the roughcast clean. Where the suburbs stride into the country nothing is more marked than the contrast between the neatly white-washed farms and cottages and the dirty harling of the new houses. Huge sums of public money have been expended on these schemes. Why has there been no insistence by the Health Department on the employment of qualified designers ? For Glasgow with 67,000 houses to build, a Christopher Wren would not be too highly skilled an official. Readers of the *Parentalia* will not require to be reminded of that great man's foresight. With such a programme before him, his first care would have been to open new quarries wherever freestone was available and arrange for the production of attractive facing bricks. He would also have balanced his schemes between country cottages and city tenements. To-day, such foresight seems to be utterly absent and *laissez faire* has proved a poor substitute.

These words are not lightly written. The writer realizes that criticism is easy and that the task which confronts the public authorities is as difficult as it is colossal. He also knows that they and their officers are as anxious as he that the task should be carried out well. It is for the use of the trained ability ready to hand that he pleads. A comfortable house need not be ugly. It need not cost more than an ugly one. Nor need it stand in an ugly street. If we have not learnt from the industrial town and the mining village the disadvantage of a life starved of beauty, we are incapable of learning anything.

Happily one can conclude this jeremiad on a more hopeful note than would have been possible a year ago. Here and there a house or a group of cottages may be seen built with good materials from good designs. Let the reader note that they are invariably the work of a trained architect. One brickwork, at least, in the west of Scotland is turning out a good facing brick. In Edinburgh and Aberdeen, stone is beginning to come back to its own. In Edinburgh there has been a courageous effort on the part of the City Architect to impart to the new municipal tenements the design and texture of Scots buildings. In this difficult enterprise he has already achieved a large measure of success. No one would expect a perfect formula to be evolved at the first attempt. In Glasgow, the lay-out of the most recent schemes shows a marked improvement. It is at last realized that the creation of a new suburb entails more than the mere erection of rows of houses—that the indefinite extension of a large city, without any attempt to preserve the beauty of the countryside or provide space for recreation, can end in nothing but discontent and calamity. Given vision and expert guidance, these welcome beginnings may yet result in new centres of which Scotland can be proud.

In a land of hills and rivers bridges play an important part. There are many fine BRIDGES (116) in Scotland but they differ little from those in England. Tradition credits Devorgilla, wife of John Balliol and foundress of Sweetheart Abbey, with building a bridge over the Nith at Dumfries in the thirteenth century. The existing bridge is called by her name, but the first bridge is known to have been of wood. Some of its timbers may survive below the water level. The fifteenth-century bridges, such as the Brig of Stirling and Brig of Earn, have semicircular arches, often ribbed, a fairly steep rise to the centre and deep cutwaters carried up to form shelters for pedestrians. The longer bridges, such as the Brig o' Dee at Aberdeen and Guard Bridge over the Eden in Fife, are quite flat. The road development of the eighteenth century naturally entailed the erection of numerous bridges. In many of these, open balustrades took the place of parapets and the piers were often marked by obelisks and vases. Of this fanciful type there are good examples at Aberfeldy and at Inveraray and Glenshira. The nineteenth century bridges were the work of engineers. They are plain structures, very carefully and durably built and either flat or nicely graded. Their charm, like that of all good engineering work, lies in what would now be called their 'stream lines'. Rennie's bridge at Kelso is one of the best. Conon Bridge is a typical example. At one moment, the existence of all these old bridges seemed to be threatened by the demands of road construction, and if local authorities had been left to themselves it is doubtful whether any would have been spared. Fortunately, the Ministry of Transport is alive to their value and, where a grant is given, makes sure, as every grant-giving department should, that public money is not used to finance acts of vandalism. Many of the old bridges have been retained and widened. Where this cannot be done, the old bridges have been kept alongside the new and, where bye-passes are made, still serve for local traffic. The designs for the more important new bridges are submitted to the Fine Art Commission. Special care has been taken about those on the new arterial roads. On the old Highland road between Perth and Inverness experiments were made in ultra-modern bridge construction, with results which have kept the critics busy ever since. Time will show whether these new ideas were sound or unsound. That the ferro-concrete bridge is capable of great beauty no one will deny who has seen one, slim and daring, leap a deep ravine or even one of low level, like that at MONTROSE (117), carrying a first-class road across a broad stretch of water. The unpleasant cement surface has hitherto been a difficulty, which even bush-hammering has not quite solved. There is much to be said for surfacing with stone. This method has been extensively employed on the new road from Glasgow to Inverness by Glencoe. The series of bridges between Ballachulish and Inverness, designed by a first-rate architect associated with a first-rate engineer, are both beautiful and appropriate.

116   DEVORGIL'S BRIDGE, DUMFRIES
STIRLING BRIDGE
SHIRA BRIDGE, ARGYLL

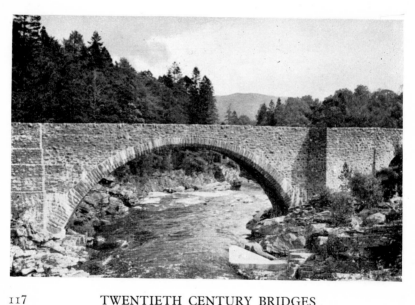

TWENTIETH CENTURY BRIDGES
Above: Montrose
Below: Glenmoriston

GARDENS

That at GLENMORISTON (117), a bold concrete structure faced with stone rubble, fits admirably into a glorious landscape. These bridges reflect great credit on the County Council of Inverness-shire, who were the first to make use of this happy combination of talents.

GARDENS lie outside the scope of this book, but a brief note on the subject may be useful, since the setting of a building is scarcely less important than the building itself and equally the concern of the architect. Unfortunately it is apt to undergo frequent alteration through changes of fashion and the whims of successive owners.

The fifteenth and sixteenth century towers had, as we have seen, walled enclosures attached to them, often of considerable size, with buildings which eked out the scanty accommodation in the tower itself and provided shelter for horses and cattle. Such enclosures may still be seen at Dunnottar and Craignethan though in most places they have disappeared. It is unlikely that they were used as gardens. There were gardens and orchards from an early period, but they were outside the wall.

The earliest piece of garden design which

survives in Scotland is the King's Knot, below Stirling Castle. This mound, attractively shaped into banks and terraces, may have been the central feature of a larger lay-out. It probably goes back to the reign of James V. It is now covered with turf, but may once have been decked with trees, hedges and flowers in the manner recommended in the earliest gardening books. At Dirleton there is a garden wall with recesses which seems to date from the late sixteenth century and a circular dovecote of about the same age. No feudal lord's establishment was complete without a dovecote. It was his privilege to let his pigeons feed on his neighbours' crops as well as his own. Nor were the ecclesiastical lords behind the temporal. A dovecote of similar design marks an angle of the Abbey wall at Crossraguel. The later dovecotes are usually square with lean-to roofs and crowsteps. But we are straying from the garden.

At EDZELL (119) there is a very complete walled garden dating from 1604. It is a thing which everyone who wishes to visualize life at that period should see. The walls are decorated on the garden side with pilasters which divide them into compartments containing alternately a single large recess for flowers, with a carved panel above, and a chequered arrangement of smaller recesses in which no doubt blue and white blossoms represented the fesse chequé of the Lindsays. Above the latter are the Lindsay stars, the centre of each being pierced to make nesting places for birds. All the flower recesses are hollowed to hold earth. The wall is also embellished with an interesting set of carved panels of Planetary Deities, Cardinal Virtues and Liberal Arts. The designs are taken from German woodcuts of the period. The Castle stands at the corner of the garden. At another corner there is a charming little house and at another a well with the remains of a bath house. This delightful place, which belongs to Lord Dalhousie, has been well cared for and always accessible. It is now in the custody of H.M. Office of Works, which has reconstituted the garden in the formal manner of the period.

We have already, at Hatton and Melville, seen fine lay-outs of the late seventeenth century. At Barncluith, near Hamilton, a smaller but fascinating garden descends with steep terraces to the wooded gorge of the river Avon. Its garden house, a gem of its kind, seems to date from the eighteenth century. The terraces and a fountain are probably older. At Dalzell in the same neighbourhood there is another terraced garden sloping down to a deep glen. It is partly old and partly designed by the late Lord Hamilton and Robert Billings on the lines of Edzell and Barncluith.

At ELLON (93) in Aberdeenshire there is a splendid terrace below the old castle and a fine sundial. At Newbattle Abbey, Drummond Castle and Drumlanrig, there are formal gardens on the grand scale which were mainly the work of nineteenth century ladies and their gardeners, though fine old sundials are evidence of earlier attempts to embellish these beautiful places. The garden designs of the nineteenth century were very good—much better than the architecture. It was while they were being carried out that Scotland earned the reputation, which she still holds, of being a country of fine gardens and good gardeners.

APPENDIX I

The Ancient Monuments Acts, 1913 and 1931, empower the Commissioner of Works to draw up from time to time lists of ancient monuments of national importance. In this task he is advised by the Ancient Monuments Boards for England, Scotland and Wales.

When a monument is scheduled, the owner is informed of the fact and warned that he may not remove or alter the monument without giving three months' notice to the Commissioners. This gives time for the project to be discussed. Should agreement not be reached, the Commissioners have power (if the monument is reported by the Advisory Boards to be in danger) to issue what is called a Preservation Order for its protection. This order is valid for twenty-one months, and, if confirmed by Parliament within that time, becomes permanent.

The Commissioners are also empowered to take over the custody of monuments offered by their owners. Where this is done, the Commissioners accept full responsibility for the care of the monument, though it remains the property of the owner. The ability of the Commissioners to take monuments over is limited by the amount of the grant voted by Parliament for their maintenance.

The Commissioners also have power to acquire monuments by purchase, gift or bequest and to contribute towards the maintenance of monuments belonging to other parties. Here again action is limited by the funds available.

The powers described in the last paragraph are equally conferred on Local Authorities, *i.e.* County Councils and Borough Councils. It is clearly the intention of the Acts that monuments other than those of national importance should be the care of Local Authorities and they are empowered to draw on the rates for this purpose. This section has been practically a dead letter in Scotland.

The amending Act of 1931 gives the Commissioners power to make what are called Preservation Schemes to protect the amenity of monuments threatened by any injurious use of the adjoining ground. Local Authorities already have that power under the Town Planning Acts.

Churches used for divine service are excluded from the operation of the Acts. So are all houses inhabited by others than caretakers. These are very severe limitations.

Within their restricted sphere the Acts have achieved much good work. We are concerned here with buildings only. It will be seen from the list which follows that two hundred and seventy-four buildings have been scheduled up to date in Scotland. The number of other entries in the schedule is over a thousand, mostly pre-historic monuments, but including also sections of the Roman Wall, certain historic landmarks and many fine carved crosses and tombstones. As the prehistoric entries often include a large number of items, the total number of monuments protected must be very large.

The weakest spot in the system is that the 'protection' is far from complete, consisting frequently of no more than a notice board and a fence. Without an army of inspectors it would be impossible to keep every isolated monument under regular supervision and the attempt to achieve the same object by voluntary local correspondents in return for a small gratuity has not so far covered the ground anything like completely. Those who have been keen enough to take on this rather thankless job are performing a very useful and very necessary national service. Buildings have fared better. The Commissioners have very rightly abstained from undertaking the guardianship of buildings to which they cannot do full justice, but all those for which they are responsible are in good order and in all the more important there are caretakers.

Without further legislation a great advance could be made if (1) the grant on which the Commissioners work were substantially increased, and (2) Local Authorities would take the part assigned to them under the Acts.

Under the *Historic Buildings and Ancient Monuments Act*, 1953, Historic Buildings Councils were established to advise the Minister of Works in making grants towards the repair or maintenance of buildings of outstanding historic or architectural interest. Under the Act £350,000 is available in the year 1956-57 for repair and maintenance grants and £500,000 for five years from the National Land Fund for the acquisition of outstanding buildings.

MODERN SHOOTING LODGE

118 MODERN HOUSE   MODERN COTTAGES

EDZELL CASTLE

Below: The Walled Garden

APPENDIX II

SOME OF THE BUILDINGS SCHEDULED AS ANCIENT MONUMENTS

(A full list is published by H.M. Stationery Office)

Key to Signs

* Monuments in the charge of the Commissioners (under the provisions of the Acts).

† Monuments which are Crown property.

ABERDEENSHIRE

* Aberdeen, St. Machar's Cathedral, the ruined transepts.

Aberdeen, Bridge of Dee.

Aberdeen, Brig o' Balgownie.

Aberdeen Market Cross.

Auchindoir, St. Mary's Kirk, near Lumsden.

Corgarff Castle, near Corgarff.

* Deer Abbey, Old Deer.

* Huntly Castle.

Kincardine O'Neil Auld Kirk.

Kildrummy Castle.

* Kinkell Kirk, near Inverurie.

* Tolquhon Castle.

ANGUS

* Affleck Castle.

† Arbroath Abbey.

237

* Arbroath, Abbot's House, The Pend, Regality Tower, Cloister Garth, Frater and adjoining land.

Braikie Castle, Inverkeilor.

† Brechin Cathedral, Round Tower.

† Brechin, Maison Dieu Chapel.

† Broughty Castle.

* Claypotts Castle.

* Edzell Castle.

Ethie, 'St. Murdoch's Chapel,' 700 yards E. of South Mains, near Inverkeilor.

* Restenneth Priory.

ARGYLL

Aray Bridge, near Inveraray.

* Carnassarie Castle, Kilmartin.

Shira Bridge, near Inveraray.

Dunollie Castle, near Oban.

Dunstaffnage Castle (uninhabited portions).

* Eilean Mor, St. Cormac's Chapel, W. coast of South Knapdale.

Gylen Castle, Kerrera, near Oban.

* Inch Kenneth Chapel and sculptured stones, Loch na Keal, Mull.

Iona Nunnery.

Iona, St. Oran's Chapel.

Kilmartin Castle.

* Kilmory Chapel, South Knapdale.

Kilneuair ruined church, near Ford, Loch Awe.

Oronsay Priory.

* Sween Castle, North Knapdale.

Tarbert Castle.

AYRSHIRE

Alloway, Auld Brig o' Doon.

Alloway Kirk, Ayr.

Auchans, near Dundonald.

Ayr, Auld Brig o' Ayr.

Ayr Citadel, parts of.

Busbie Castle, Crosshouse.

* Crossraguel Abbey.

Cumnock Market Cross.

Dalquharran Castle, New Dailly.

Dundonald Castle.

Glengarnock Castle, near Kilbirnie.

Kilwinning Abbey.

* Largs, Skelmorlie Aisle.

Loch Doon Castle.

BANFFSHIRE

* Balvenie Castle.

Boyne Castle, $1\frac{1}{4}$ miles E. of Portsoy.

Deskford Old Kirk.

BERWICKSHIRE

Bunkle, Old Kirk, near Lintlaw, Chirnside.

Cockburnspath Market Cross.

* Dryburgh Abbey.

Edrom, Old Kirk (Norman doorway).

BUTESHIRE

Rothesay Castle.

APPENDIX II

CAITHNESS
Girnigo Castle and Castle Sinclair.
Keiss Castle.
Latheron, Bell Tower.
Thurso, St. Peter's Kirk.

CLACKMANNANSHIRE
Alloa, Old Parish Kirk.
Alloa Tower, near Alloa.
Castle Campbell, Dollar.
Clackmannan Tower.
Sauchie (or Devon) Tower, Alloa.
Tullibody, old bridge one mile W. of.
Tullibody, Old Parish Kirk.

DUMBARTONSHIRE
Dumbarton Castle.
Dumbarton, Glencairn Greit Tenement, High Street.

DUMFRIES-SHIRE
Amisfield Tower.
Caerlaverock Castle.
Comlongan Castle.
Dumfries, 'Devorgilla' Bridge.
Fourmerkland Tower, near Irongray Station, Holy-
    wood.
Frenchland Tower, near Moffat.
Torthorwald Castle.

EAST LOTHIAN
Abbey Bridge, Haddington.
Barnes Castle ('The Vaults'), Athelstaneford.

SCHEDULED BUILDINGS

* Dirleton Castle.

Dunbar Castle and Fort.

Dunbar, dovecot (remains of Red Friars Monastery).

* Dunglass Chapel (Collegiate Kirk), near Cockburnspath.

East Linton Bridge.

Elphinstone Tower, Tranent.

Falside Castle, near Tranent.

Fenton Tower, Kingston, near North Berwick.

Gullane, St. Andrews Kirk.

Haddington, Nungate Bridge.

* Haddington, St. Martin's Kirk.

† Haddington, St. Mary's Kirk.

* Hailes Castle, East Linton.

Innerwick Castle.

Keith Kirk, Keith Marischal, near Humbie.

Luffness Convent, Aberlady.

North Berwick Nunnery.

Ormiston Hall, St. Giles Kirk, near Ormiston.

Ormiston Market Cross.

* Preston Cross, Prestonpans.

Prestonpans, Old Hamilton House (Magdalen's House).

Preston Tower (or Castle) and dovecot, Prestonpans.

Redhouse, near Longniddry.

Saltcoats Castle and dovecot, Gullane.

Seton Collegiate Kirk.

Stenton, Old Parish Kirk.

Stoneypath Tower, Garvald.

* Tantallon Castle.

Tynninghame House, St. Baldred's Kirk.

Yester Castle and the Goblin Ha', near Gifford.

FIFE

Abdie Old Kirk, Lindores.

Aberdour Castle.

Aberdour, Old Parish Kirk.‡

Balgonie Castle, near Markinch.

Ballinbreich Castle, near Newburgh.

Balmerino Abbey.

Bandon Tower, ¾ mile N.W. of Balfarg, near Markinch.

Collairnie Castle, Dunbog.

Craighall Castle, near Ceres.

Creich Castle and dovecot.

Cruivie Castle, South Straiton, Lucklawhill, near Leuchars.

* Culross Abbey.

* Culross Palace.

Dairsie Bridge, ¾ mile S. of Dairsie.

Dairsie Castle, ¾ mile S. of Dairsie.

Dalgety Bay, St. Bridget's Kirk, near Aberdour.

† Dunfermline Abbey.

† Dunfermline Palace.

Falkland Palace.

Guard Bridge, St. Andrews.

* Inchcolm Abbey.

* Inchcolm Abbey, hog-backed monument near.

Lindores Abbey, Newburgh.

‡ Used for Ecclesiastical purposes.

Lochore Castle.
Lordscairnie Castle, 3 miles N.W. of Cupar.
Mountquhanie Castle, near Kilmany.
Pittarthie Castle, near Dunino.
Ravenscraig Castle, Kirkcaldy.
† Rosyth Castle.
Rosyth Old Kirk, near Limekilns, Dunfermline.
* St. Andrews, Blackfriars Chapel.
† St. Andrews Castle.
† St. Andrews Cathedral and Precincts.
St. Andrews, St. Leonard's Kirk.
† St. Andrews. St. Mary's Kirk, Kirkhill.
St. Andrews, West Port.
Scotstarvit Tower, Ceres.
Tulliallan Castle, Kincardine.
Tulliallan Old Parish Kirk, Kincardine.

INVERNESS-SHIRE

† Beauly Priory.
Eilean Tirrim Castle (Castle Tioram), Loch Moidart.
Inverlochy Castle, Fort William.
Kiessimul Castle, Castle Bay, Barra.
Macdonald, Flora, remains of her house, No. 1,
  Airidh Mhuilinn, South Uist.
* Rodel or Rowdil, St. Clement's Church, Harris.
Skeabost Island, 'St. Columba's Church' and other
  ecclesiastical remains, Skeabost Bridge, Skye.
Trumpan Church, near Hallin, Vaternish, Skye.
* Urquhart Castle.

KINCARDINESHIRE

Brig o' Dye, on Cairn o' Mount Road.
Dunnottar Castle.
Fiddes Castle.

KINROSS-SHIRE

Aldie Castle, 2 miles S.E. of Crook of Devon.
Arnot Tower, near Scotlandwell.
* Burleigh Castle.
Dowhill Castle, near Cleish.
Loch Leven Castle.
St. Serf's Priory, St. Serf's Island, Loch Leven.

KIRKCUDBRIGHTSHIRE

* Cardoness Castle.
* Carsluith Castle.
Drumcoltran Tower, Kirkgunzeon.
† Dundrennan Abbey.
Hills Tower, near Lochfoot.‡
* Lincluden College.
* McClellan's Castle, Kirkcudbright.
* Orchardton Tower.
Rusko Castle, Anwoth.
* Sweetheart Abbey.
* Threave Castle, Castle Douglas.

LANARKSHIRE

Bothwell Bridge.
* Bothwell Castle.

‡ Occupied as dwelling-house.

SCHEDULED BUILDINGS

Craignethan Castle, Lesmahagow.

Douglas, St. Bride's Chapel.

Glasgow, 'Provand's Lordship' (St. Nicholas' Hospital), No. 3, Castle Street.

Glasgow, the Tolbooth Steeple.

Hallbar Tower, Carluke.

Lanark, Old Bridge.

Lanark, St. Kentigern's Kirk.

MIDLOTHIAN

Brunston Castle, near Penicuik.

Cairns Castle, Harperrig.

Cockpen, Old Parish Kirk, near Bonnyrigg.

* Crichton Castle.

Dalkeith, choir of Collegiate Kirk of St. Nicholas (parish church).

† Edinburgh Castle.

Edinburgh, Colinton Castle.

Edinburgh, Craiglockhart Castle.

Edinburgh, Craigmillar Castle.

Edinburgh, Cramond Old Bridge.

Edinburgh, Cramond Tower.

Edinburgh, Dovecot, Dovecot Road, Corstorphine.

Edinburgh, Liberton Tower.

Maiden Bridge, Newbattle Abbey, near Dalkeith.

Musselburgh Old Bridge.

Rosslyn Castle, Lasswade.

Temple Old Kirk.

Woolmet House, Edmonstone.

MORAYSHIRE
    Coxton Tower.
* Duffus Castle.
* Duffus, St. Peter's Kirk and Parish Cross.
† Elgin Cathedral.
    Kinloss Abbey.
    Pluscarden Priory, near Elgin.
    Spynie Castle.

NAIRN
    Inshoch Castle, near Auldearn.

ORKNEY
* Egilsay Church.
* Eynhallow Church.
* Kirkwall, the Bishop's and Earl's Palaces.
* Noltland Castle, Westray.
    Orphir, remains of circular church of.
* Pierowall Church, Westray.
* St. Mary's Chapel, Viera.
* Westray Westside Church.

PEEBLESSHIRE
    Drochil Castle.
    Neidpath Castle.
* Peebles, the Cross Kirk.

PERTHSHIRE
* Abernethy Round Tower and symbol stone.
    Doune, Bridge of Teith.
    Doune Castle.

† Dunkeld Cathedral.
Earn, Old Bridge of.
* Elcho Castle, Rhynd.
* Huntingtower, Perth.
* Inchmahome Priory.
Kinclaven Castle.
Muthill Kirk Tower.
Spittal of Glenshee, bridge at.
Stobhall, near Stanley.
Tullibardine Kirk.

RENFREWSHIRE
Barr Castle, near Lochwinnoch.
Castle Semple Collegiate Kirk, near Lochwinnoch.
Crookston Castle, near Paisley.
* Newark Castle, Port Glasgow.

ROSS AND CROMARTY
Castle Craig, Black Isle.
† Fortrose Cathedral and Precincts.

ROXBURGHSHIRE
Cessford Castle, near Morebattle.
Ferniehirst Castle, near Jedburgh.
* Hermitage Castle, Castleton.
Jedburgh, Canongate Bridge.
* Jedburgh Abbey.
Jedburgh, Queen Mary's House.
* Kelso Abbey.
* Melrose Abbey.
Smailholm Tower.

APPENDIX II

SELKIRKSHIRE
  Kirkhope Tower, near Ettrick Bridge.

STIRLINGSHIRE
  * Cambuskenneth Abbey.
  † Stirling, Argyll's Lodging.
  † Stirling, Bothwell's House.
  † Stirling Castle.
  † Stirling, King's Knott.
  * Stirling, 'Marr's Wark'.
  * Stirling, Old Bridge.

SUTHERLAND
  Ardvreck Castle, near Inchnadamph.

WEST LOTHIAN
  † Blackness Castle.
  † Linlithgow Palace.
  Old Dundas Castle and sundial, near South Queensferry.
  Staneyhill Tower, near Abercorn.
  * Torphichen Preceptory.

WIGTOWNSHIRE
  Craigcaffie Tower, near Stranraer.
  * Glenluce Abbey.
  * St. Ninian's Chapel, Isle of Whithorn.
  * Whithorn Priory.

ZETLAND
  * Scalloway Castle.

APPENDIX III

Note on the Origin of the Pointed Arch

This note is added for the benefit of readers who are curious about the change from the round to the pointed arch. An examination of the buildings themselves shows that the pointed form first became necessary in the construction of the groined vault.

The earliest churches in France were modelled on the buildings left by the Romans in that country. The nave, if vaulted in stone, had a plain barrel vault, which is simply a continuous arch or tunnel resting on the side walls. The plain barrel was later strengthened at intervals by supporting arches, carried on pilasters attached to the walls. This form of vault is open to two serious objections. It exerts a strong outward thrust which necessitates walls of great thickness and it makes the upper part of the building very dark. The first difficulty was not felt by the Romans, as their vaults were constructed of concrete which hardened into so solid a mass that it only exerted a downward pressure. The other they overcame by constructing transverse vaults at right angles to the main vault which admitted of the windows being carried as high as the crown of the vault. The angles where the vaults cut one another are known as groins, and a roof composed of intersecting vaults is described as groined. The use of concrete was apparently unknown to the French church builders. Their vaults were built with stones and mortar. But they were able to make groined roofs by constructing arched ribs at the groins against which the comparatively small panels of intervening masonry abutted. The roof was divided into sections by the supporting arches already mentioned. Each section had its own intersecting vault and the groin ribs sprang from the same pilasters as the supporting arches. The weight and thrust of the roof were thus concentrated at certain definite points instead of being spread over the whole length of the wall. This is the essential principle of Gothic architecture. At these points the walls were strengthened by buttresses, corresponding to the pilasters inside. The walls between these points could now be diminished in thickness and freely pierced with windows, an opportunity of which the medieval artists made admirable use.

So long as the vaulting compartments remained square, the round arch satisfied all the requirements of this arrangement. But when the width of the nave was increased and the compartments became oblong, the use of a round arch for the narrow end of the oblong became extremely inconvenient. If it sprang from the same point as the groins and the wide supporting arches which cross the nave, it was too low and the vault remained very dark. If it was stilted—that is, if the sides were carried up straight to raise the arch to the full height of the nave—it became structurally unsound. This difficulty was overcome by replacing the round arch by one of pointed form, whose width and height could be exactly adjusted to the needs of the case. The clerestory windows being bounded by this arch naturally followed its curve. Once this form of arch had been adopted, its flexibility was found so convenient that it soon drove the other out of use in France and England. The reader must not assume that the pointed arch was unknown before it was put to this use. It had long been used in the eastern churches and the Provençal builders had pointed their barrel vaults in order to lessen the outward thrust.

APPENDIX IV

COLLEGIATE CHURCHES OF SCOTLAND
(*from Walcot's 'Ancient Churches of Scotland'*)

DIOCESE OF ST. ANDREWS
Crail.
Foulis.
Methven.
St. Salvator, St. Andrews.
Kirkheugh, St. Andrews.
St. Leonard, St. Andrews.

DIOCESE OF ABERDEEN
King's College, Aberdeen.
St. Nicholas, Aberdeen.
St. Mary, Cullen.
Kennethmont.

DIOCESE OF ARGYLL
Kilmun (on the Holy
     Loch).

DIOCESE OF BRECHIN
Guthrie.

DIOCESE OF EDINBURGH
Corstorphine.

Crichton.
Dalkeith.
Dirleton.
Dunbar.
Dunglass.
Holy Trinity, Edinburgh.
St. Giles, Edinburgh.
St. Mary (Kirk o' Fields)
     Edinburgh.
St. Michael, Linlithgow.
Restalrig.
Rosslyn.
Seton.
Chapel Royal, Stirling.
Yester.

DIOCESE OF GALLOWAY
Lincluden.

DIOCESE OF GLASGOW
Biggar.
Bothwell.

Carnwath.

Dumbarton.

Ss. Mary and Anne, Glasgow.

Hamilton.

Kilmaurs.

Maybole.

St. Andrew, Peebles.

Semple or Lochwinnoch.

DIOCESE OF MORAY

Abernethy.

DIOCESE OF ROSS

Tain.

INDEX

INDEX

INDEX

INDEX

INDEX

INDEX

INDEX

INDEX

PRINTED IN GREAT BRITAIN BY
GILMOUR AND DEAN LTD., GLASGOW AND LONDON